Diesterwegs Neusprachliche Arbeitsmittel Englisch

Bernhard Stentenbach

Lernwortschatz zur englischen Textarbeit

Diesterweg

Unter Mitarbeit von Eva Markert

Sprachliche Beratung: Richard Lord

Druck A[13] / Jahr 2012
Alle Drucke der Serie A sind im Unterricht parallel verwendbar.

Umschlaggestaltung: Reckels und Schneider-Reckels, Wiesbaden
Satz: fotosatz griesheim GmbH, Griesheim
Druck und Bindung: Westermann Druck GmbH, Zwickau

ISBN 978-3-425-04119-3

VORWORT

Der vorliegende „Lernwortschatz zur englischen Textarbeit“ ist die adaptierte Fassung des völlig neu entwickelten „Lernwortschatzes zur französischen Textarbeit“. Er entspricht in Inhalt und Aufbau den Anforderungen, die in den neuen Lehrplänen der Bundesländer an die Textarbeit von Klasse 10 bis zum Abitur gestellt werden. Er berücksichtigt gezielt die praktischen Bedürfnisse der Benutzer bei der Textarbeit im Unterricht und bei den Klausuren.

Der neue „Lernwortschatz“ gibt umfassende Hilfen für die Behandlung aller wesentlichen Textsorten (literarische / fiktionale und nicht-literarische / nicht-fiktionale Texte).
Ein besonderes Kapitel ist der Abfassung eines Textkommentars gewidmet. Es enthält alle wichtigen Ausdrücke zur persönlichen Stellungnahme sowie einen speziellen Wortschatz zum Textzusammenhang, der hinsichtlich der Realisierung von Satzverknüpfung und Textstruktur eine große Hilfe darstellt.
In einem abschließenden Kapitel wird ein Diskussionswortschatz angeboten, der die wichtigsten Ausdrücke und Wendungen für das Unterrichtsgespräch im Rahmen der Textarbeit enthält.

Der neue „Lernwortschatz“ hat den Charakter eines echten Lernwörterbuchs, das folgende Vorteile aufweist:

- Zu allen wesentlichen englischen Wörtern und Ausdrücken wird in der rechten Spalte die deutsche Bedeutung angegeben. Die betreffenden englischen Wörter sind kursiv gedruckt.
- Aus der Fülle der englischen Ausdrücke wurde ein sog. unverzichtbares Grundvokabular ausgewählt, das bei der Textarbeit ab Klasse 10 eingesetzt werden kann. Das Grundvokabular ist durch Punkte (•) am Rand gekennzeichnet. Auf dieser Basis kann der Schüler eigenständig im Laufe der Jahrgangsstufen 11 – 13 entsprechend seiner speziellen Bedürfnisse nach und nach sein individuelles Textbesprechungsvokabular erweitern.
- Ein systematisches Lernen und gezieltes Wiederholen der Ausdrücke wird dadurch erleichtert, dass in der Anordnung des Lernvokabulars das Wichtige vom weniger Wichtigen unterschieden wird, d.h.
  - die in einem Ausdruck als Beispiel hinzugefügten inhaltlichen Elemente sind in Klammern gesetzt,
  - die zu einem bestimmten Ausdruck hinzugefügten kontextualisierten Beispiele sind generell eingerückt.

  Dies bedeutet:
  - dass der Benutzer / die Benutzerin sich beim Lernen nur auf die eigentlichen Ausdrücke (ohne die inhaltlichen Elemente und ohne die kontextualisierten Satzbeispiele) konzentrieren kann,
  - dass er / sie jedoch bei Bedarf die Möglichkeit hat, die hinzugefügten inhaltlichen Elemente und kontextualisierten Satzbeispiele mitzulernen, da diese eine Bereicherung seines / ihres Ausdrucksvermögens darstellen.

Ein deutsch-englisches Stichwortverzeichnis erschließt das Vokabular der Textbesprechung vom Deutschen her. Es umfasst die wichtigsten deutschen Wörter und Ausdrücke und ihre englischen Entsprechungen unter Hinweis auf die entsprechenden Stellen im „Lernwortschatz“.

Bernhard Stentenbach

INHALTSVERZEICHNIS

1. DER TEXT *(the text)*

1.1. Die Textquelle *(the source)*

• The *text is taken from* the magazine "..."	*Text; ... stammt aus*
This text is taken from an article *published* in ("The Times").	*veröffentlichen*
• This text is taken from the book "..." (written) by ... / is taken from a novel, which was *published* in (1992).	
• This text is *an extract from* the novel "..." by ...	*ein Auszug aus*

1.2. Der Titel / die Überschrift *(the title, the heading, the headline)*

• The *title* of the text is ...	*Titel*
• The *heading* of the *chapter* is ...	*Überschrift; Kapitel*
• The *headline* of the article is ...	*Überschrift*
The text is *entitled* "..."	*betitelt*
The title *states* / *indicates* *the subject.* / *the topic.*	*das Thema angeben*
the *subject-matter* of the text	*Stoff*
The title is followed by a *subtitle*. / The *subheading* puts the subject more exactly.	*Untertitel*
A possible heading for the third part is ...	

1.3. Das Thema *(the subject, the theme, the topic)*

• The text *deals with* / *is about* pollution. / the situation of young people.	*handeln von*
• *The text says that ...*	*Im Text steht, dass ...*
The theme of the text is "War".	*Das Thema des Textes ist ...*
• The text is about a *current* problem. / a subject *of topical importance.*	*aktuell*
The text *deals with* / *is about* *a* serious social *problem.* / *the question* of security.	*ein Problem behandeln*

1.4. Der Adressat *(the reader, the addressee)*

The text *is intended for* readers who are interested in ... / The text *addresses* people who want to be informed about ...	*sich wenden an*
• The text *appeals to* the average reader.	*appellieren an*

1.5. Der Aufbau / die Gliederung *(the structure / the composition)*

(The following expressions are useful for writing abstracts.)

1.5.1. Grobeinteilung *(a rough analysis of the structure)*

• the *composition* of the text	*Aufbau, Gliederung*
• The text *comprises* three parts. / four *paragraphs.* / five *sections.*	*umfassen* / *Abschnitt*
The text *is composed of* / *consists of* / *divides into* — three parts. / four paragraphs. / five sections.	*bestehen aus* / *unterteilt sich in*
In the text three different parts can be *distinguished.*	*unterscheiden*
The second part can be *subdivided* into three *smaller parts.* / into three *subsections.*	*unterteilen* / *Unterabschnitt*
The *main part* of the text consists of ...	*Hauptteil*

1.5.2. Genauere Einteilung mit Thema *(a more detailed analysis including the theme)*

• The first part *runs from line ... (up) to line ...*	*geht von Zeile ... bis Zeile*
The second paragraph / The third section — comprises the lines ... / begins in line ... and ends in line ...	
In the first part the *author* / the *writer* deals with ...	*Verfasser(in)*
One can *draw parallels between* the four parts of the text.	*Parallelen ziehen*
• *At the beginning* of the text / *First* / *First of all* / *In the first place* — the author ...	*zuerst*
The text *begins with* / *starts with* — the presentation of the problem. / the presentation of the problem in question.	*... beginnt mit*
The author *begins by* saying ...	
The author *starts the text with* ...	
• *Then* / *After that* / *Afterwards* — the reader learns ... / the author deals with ...	*dann, danach*
• *At the end* of the text / *Finally* / *Lastly* — the writer ...	*zum Schluss*

The text *ends with ...* / *concludes with ...*	*... endet mit*
The author concludes / finishes / closes the text by *stating ...*	*behaupten*
declaring ...	*erklären*
asserting ...	*versichern*
The text concludes in a rather *optimistic* tone.	*optimistisch*
pessimistic	*pessimistisch*

1.5.3. Einleitung – Hauptteil – Schluss eines fiktionalen Textes *(Exposition – development – denouement of a fictional text /* Einleitung – Hauptteil – Schluss eines Sachtextes *(introduction – main part – conclusion of a non-fictional text)*

In the *exposition* of a short story, the author gives information on / about the characters.	*Einleitung (z. B. einer Kurzgeschichte)*
• The first part *forms the introduction.*	*... bildet die Einleitung*
The first paragraph *is a kind of introduction.*	*... ist eine Art Einleitung*
In the introduction the author *points out* / *presents* the problem. / the subject of the text.	*darlegen*
The parts 2 to 4 / The paragraphs 2 to 4 form / constitute the *main part* of the text.	*Hauptteil*
• The main part runs from line ... to line ... / comprises the *chapters* 2 to 4.	*Kapitel*
In this part the author *develops* / *explains* his idea of liberty. / ...	*entwickeln*
• In this part the author *gives his opinion of / about ...*	*sich äußern zu*
• *The main idea* / *The principal idea* / *The central idea* of that part is ...	*Hauptgedanke*
In the *denouement* of the story, the conflict is solved.	*Ausgang, Lösung*
The story has a happy *ending*.	*Ende (einer Geschichte)*
In the final part / *In the conclusion* the author states that ...	*Schlussteil*
• The final part is a *summary* of ...	*Zusammenfassung*
In the final part the author gives a summary of ... / *summarizes ...*	*zusammenfassen*
• In the final part the author *comes to* / *draws* *the conclusion* that ...	*zu dem Schluss kommen*

1.5.4. Textstelle *(a passage of a text)*

• In this *passage* the author says that ...	*Textstelle*
• This passage | *shows* | the author's intentions. | *reveals* |	*enthüllen*
This passage | forms a *transition* to ...	*Überleitung*
| *leads up to* ...	*überleiten zu*

1.5.5. Zusammenfassung *(summary)*

The text can be summarized in a few words.	
The *contents* of the text can be summarized in a few sentences.	*Inhalt*
The contents of the text can be summarized as follows: ...	

1.6. Der Charakter des Textes *(the character of the text)*

The text is easy to understand.	
• It is a *dialogue.*	*Dialog*
The text contains *narrative* passages and parts written in dialogue.	*erzählend*
• The text is | a sort of | *report.* | a kind of | *account.*	*Bericht*
It is an *autobiographic(al)* account.	*autobiografisch*
It contains | *comic(al)* | elements.	*komisch*
| *humorous* |	*humoristisch*
The *comic effect* of the text | is mainly produced by ...	*Komik*
| *consists in (the fact that)* ...	*... besteht in*
The *humour* in the text *is* especially *apparent* in ...	*Humor; sich zeigen*
The text | has a *tendency* towards | *irony.*	*Tendenz; Ironie*
| shows a tendency towards | *satire.*	*Satire*
| Irony | *shows* in ... | Satire | *manifests itself* in ...	*sich zeigen*
• The text is written in an *ironic(al)* tone.	*ironisch*
It contains *satiric(al)* elements.	*satirisch*
The text is a *parody* which is supposed to illustrate	*Parodie*
the *weaknesses* of a person.	*Schwächen*
The text gives a *caricature* of ...	*Karikatur*
It is above all the *fantastical* aspect of the story	*fantastisch*
• which *awakens* the reader's *interest.*	*Interesse wecken*
The tone of the text is rather pessimistic.	

1.7. Die Geschichte – die Handlung – das Handlungsgefüge *(the story - the action - the plot)*

The author *made up* the story.	*erfinden, sich ausdenken*
• It is a *fictional* story which is not based on reality.	*fiktional, ausgedacht*

• The story is told from *the point of view* of a child.	*Standpunkt*
the perspective	*Perspektive*
• The ending of the story is not *plausible.* / *believable.*	*glaubhaft*
• The denouement is *implausible.* / *unbelievable.*	*unglaubhaft*
improbable.	*unwahrscheinlich*
• The author relates the story from / tells the story *a remote standpoint.*	*Distanz*
in with an ironic(al) tone.	*in ironischem Ton*
• The *action* / The *plot* takes place / is set (during the Second World War). / (in an old village inn).	*Handlung*
The author does not *mention* / does not *indicate* the time when the action takes place.	*angeben*
In the introduction, place, time and characters are *given exactly.*	*genau angeben*
• The *setting of / for the action* is realistic.	*Handlungsrahmen*
unreal. / *imaginary.*	*unwirklich*
• The action is set in *reality.*	*Wirklichkeit*
in the narrator's *imagination.*	*Fantasie*
The action *develops* in several *stages.*	*verlaufen; Etappe*
• *In the course of* the action there is	*im Verlauf von*
• an *intensification* of the conflict.	*Steigerung*
The action becomes more *intense.*	*intensiv*
There are *inexplicable* phenomena.	*unerklärlich*
• *Suspense* is created because the denouement comes only in the final sentence.	*Spannung*
The author intends to arouse suspense.	
He maintains suspense throughout the story.	
Certain elements of suspense are added to the story.	
Suspense *results from* the *conflict*	*herrühren von; Konflikt*
between action and *counteraction.*	*Gegenhandlung*
... is in a difficult situation.	
• The situation is *characterized* by	*kennzeichnen*
• the *hostility* between ... and ...	*Feindschaft*
The situation seems quite *absurd* because of ...	*absurd*
The *absurdity* of the situation is *underlined* by ...	*Absurdität; betonen*
emphasized by ...	*betonen*
The situation dealt with in the description seems slightly unreal.	
• The description creates an *atmosphere* of sadness.	*Atmosphäre*
conveys a *hostile* atmosphere.	*feindlich*

This scene is typical of the *hostility* between ... and ...	*Feindseligkeit*
full of *sarcasm.*	*Sarkasmus*
In this scene comic *effects* are used.	*Effekt, Wirkung*
elements of surprise	*Überraschungsmoment*

1.8. Der Erzähler *(the narrator)*

• The story is told by a *narrator.*	*Erzähler*
The author and the narrator are not *identical.*	*identisch*
The narrator tells the story from his point of view.	
reports what he observes.	
relates the events in an objective / subjective way.	
does not always express his feelings / emotions.	
The author speaks *in the first person.*	*in der ersten Person*
• uses a *first-person narrator.*	*Ich-Erzähler*
• The first-person narrator is a *witness* to the matters he relates.	*Zeuge*
• The *third-person narrator* stands outside the story.	*Er-Erzähler*
The *omniscient* narrator knows all about the characters' thoughts, feelings and motives.	*allwissend*
The omniscient narrator is *superior to* the reader.	*überlegen*

1.9. Die Personenbeschreibung *(the characterization)*

• The *main character* / The *principal character* in the story is ...	*Hauptperson*
Another central character is ...	*eine weitere Hauptperson*
The author *characterizes* ... *(as ...)*	*jdn charakterisieren (als)*
describes ... *(as ...)*	*jdn beschreiben (als)*
... is a *hard* man.	*hart*
... has an *aggressive* temperament.	*aggressiv*
... is *intolerable.*	*unerträglich*
... has a bad character.	
• *As far as* his character *is concerned,* it can be said	*was ... betrifft*
that he is *naive* and *sentimental.*	*naiv; sentimental*
Concerning his character, it can be said that ...	*was ... betrifft*
• He has many positive *(personality) traits.* / *traits of character.* / *characteristics.*	*Charakterzug*
The *predominant* trait of his character is miserliness.	*vorherrschend*
Another essential *quality* is ...	*Eigenschaft*
• ... is mainly characterized by his *selfishness.*	*Egoismus*
... is described in a negative way.	
• His *behaviour* is marked by arrogance.	*Verhalten*
His *conduct* could be characterized as *rough.*	*Verhalten; grob*

He shows aggressive behaviour.	
A positive *aspect* / A negative aspect of his behaviour is ...	*Aspekt*
... *behaves* in an authoritarian way towards ...	*sich verhalten*
His behaviour is mainly *influenced* by hate.	*beeinflussen*
With his brutal behaviour, he wants to *assert*	*geltend machen*
• his *superiority.*	*Überlegenheit*
His behaviour is influenced by his *social* *background.* / *milieu.*	*soziales Milieu*
• ... is / ... is characterized as *indifferent to* ...	*gleichgültig gegenüber*
... reacts *indifferently* to ... / *in an indifferent way.*	*gleichgültig* (Adv.)
... shows *indifference* to ...	*Gleichgültigkeit*
His indifference becomes apparent in the fact that ...	
... is a little naive.	
... seems (to be) naive.	
... shows great *naivety.*	*Naivität*
... is a *victim* of (his own naivety).	*Opfer*
... does sth out of love for ...	
... shows *understanding* when he says that ...	*Verständnis*
... has understanding for ...	
... shows an *understanding* attitude to ...	*verständnisvoll*
• ... is / ... feels *superior* to ... because of his intelligence.	*überlegen*
... shows his superiority by saying that ...	
He considers the others (as/ to be) *inferior* to himself.	*unterlegen*
... *has* a *dislike of* ...	*Abneigung empfinden gegen*
... is *filled with* deep love for...	*erfüllt von*
... is obsessed by / with *jealousy* of his wife / her husband.	*Eifersucht*
... has a deep *mistrust* of ...	*Misstrauen*
... has a feeling of (*loneliness*).	*Einsamkeit*
... feels a *need* to talk to ...	*Bedürfnis*
... talks about his *mental sufferings.*	*seelische Leiden*
• ... shows great *sensitivity* to (the feelings of ...)	*Sensibilität*
... *lacks* sensitivity.	*... fehlt es an*
His *lack of* sensitivity is obvious.	*Mangel an*
He is *insensitive* to (the problems of ...)	*unsensibel*

• He does not show any *feelings.* / *emotion(s).*	*Gemütsbewegungen*
He does not show any *emotional reaction.*	*Gefühlsregung*
... seems to have little contact to *the people around him / her.*	*seine / ihre Umgebung*
... seems to *resign himself / herself to* the idea that ...	*sich abfinden mit*
... seems (to be) *shocked* by ...	*entsetzt*
... is incapable of understanding / ... is unable to understand somebody's *state of mind.*	*Gemütsverfassung*
is unable to *communicate* with ...	*sich austauschen*
• ... lives in a *superficial* way.	*oberflächlich*
... *arouses suspicion.*	*Misstrauen wecken*
He speaks in a *spontaneous* manner.	*spontan*
He always acts *prudently.*	*überlegt*
He reacts in a way that is ...	
the *motive* for his *actions*	*Motiv; Tat, Handlung*
• the *reason* for his actions	*Beweggrund*
the *grounds* for his actions	*(berechtigte) Gründe*
His *rash* action *makes no sense.* / *does not make (any) sense.*	*übereilt; keinen Sinn machen*
There is no sense in his rash reaction.	
... acts against his *moral principles.*	*moralische Prinzipien*
• ... is easily *impressed* by ...	*beeindrucken*
• ... is *influenced* by his environment.	*beeinflussen*
• ... *listens* too much *to* what other people say.	*hören auf*
... *cherishes the illusion* that ...	*sich der Illusion hingeben*
... has to *bear the consequences* of his actions.	*die Folgen tragen*
... *treats* the person he is talking to gently.	*behandeln*
... speaks in an *impolite* way.	*unhöflich*
... has *confidence* in (his friend).	*Vertrauen*
He is *self-confident.* / *sure of himself.*	*selbstbewusst, selbstsicher*
He lacks *self-confidence.*	*Selbstbewusstsein*
He lacks *self-assurance.*	*Selbstsicherheit*
His lack of self-confidence shows in the fact that ...	
... *is confronted with* / ... *faces* a problem. / death.	*konfrontiert sein mit*
the *confrontation* with death	*Konfrontation*
... is *the accused* in the trial.	*der / die Angeklagte*
... is *guilty* of ...	*schuldig*

... is aware of his *guilt.*	*Schuld*
... tries to *justify* his acts.	*rechtfertigen*
His *capacities* tend to be *overrated.*	*Fähigkeit; überschätzen*
His *influence* tends to be overrated.	*Einfluss*
• ... tries to *achieve* / *reach* *his aim.* / *his goal.*	*sein Ziel erreichen*
... is in a *dilemma.*	*Dilemma*
... does not know how to get out of the dilemma.	
• As to his *social position ...* / *social status ...* / *social standing ...*	*soziale Stellung*
people from different *social strata* / *levels of society*	*Gesellschaftsschichten*
his friend's *social background* / *the social class* his friend belongs to	*soziales Milieu*
He is a member of *the aristocracy.*	*die Aristokratie*
He is a member of *the upper classes.*	*die Oberschicht*
the lifestyle of *the (upper) middle class*	*die (gehobene) Mittelschicht*
He comes from a middle-class environment.	
He belongs to *the lower classes.*	*die Unterschicht*
class-conscious industrial workers	*klassenbewusst*
class-consciousness in Britain	*Klassenbewusstsein*
He wants to *rise in social class.* / *improve his social status.*	*gesellschaftlich aufsteigen*
He speaks English with a local accent. / standard English. / the Queen's English.	
His manner of speaking does not correspond with / to his *intellectual level.*	*geistiges Niveau*
• As far as his *physical appearance* / *outward appearance* is concerned ...	*Aussehen*
• ... *plays an important role.*	*eine wichtige Rolle spielen*
... plays a *secondary* role.	*untergeordnet, nebensächlich*

2. DER AUTOR *(the author, the writer)*

2.1. Die Meinung *(the opinion)*

2.1.1. Eine Meinung / Auffassung vertreten *(to be of an opinion, to hold a view)*

- The author says that ...
  The author *thinks* that ... / *believes* that ... / *has the opinion* that ... / *takes the view* that ... — *die Meinung vertreten*
- The author
- *gives* / *expresses* / *utters* / *voices* — *his (personal) opinion of* / *his (personal) view on* — *about ...* / *about ...* — *(persönliche) Meinung äußern zu*
- *According to the author ...* — *nach Meinung des Autors / der Autorin.*
- *In his opinion ...* / *In his view ...* / *To his mind ...* — *seiner Meinung nach*
  The author does not want to *change his opinion.* / The author refuses to *change his mind.* — *seine Meinung ändern*

2.1.2. Einen Standpunkt darlegen *(to explain one's point of view)*

- The author *explains* his *standpoint* — *darlegen; Standpunkt*
  with regard to ... / *in relation to ...* — *hinsichtlich*
  He *states* the viewpoint of (his adversary). — *nennen*
- He looks at the matter
  from the point of view of ... — *vom Standpunkt des ... aus*
- He *illustrates* his point of view with an example. — *veranschaulichen*
  The author's standpoint is unacceptable. / *disputable.* — *anfechtbar*

2.1.3. Eine bestimmte Einstellung haben, sich äußern *(to have a certain attitude, to make comments)*

- The author sets out his *position on ...* — *Einstellung zu* / makes his position clear.
  He takes an unacceptable / a disputable position.
  He *expresses* his personal ideas about ... — *äußern*
- He *comments on* the situation. — *sich äußern zu*
  He *makes a comment on / about ...* / *gives his opinion about / of ...* — *Stellung nehmen zu*

He | shows / presents | his *attitude* to / towards … — *Haltung, Einstellung*
This passage reveals the author's *critical* attitude to / towards … — *kritisch*

2.1.4. Eine bestimmte Vorstellung haben *(to have certain ideas about)*

- The author | explains / expresses | his *idea* / his *conception* | of (friendship). — *Vorstellung* / *Auffassung*
  His idea of (peace) is scarcely / hardly *realistic.* — *realistisch*
  He has an *unrealistic* idea of (liberty). — *unrealistisch*

2.1.5. Das Urteil, beurteilen *(the judgement, to judge)*

- to make a *judgement* on / about … — *Urteil*
  The judgement | *is based on* facts. — *basiert auf*
  | is *well-founded.* — *begründet*
  | *unfounded.* — *unbegründet*
  The author's judgements are not *objective.* — *objektiv*
  He is | *impartial.* — *unparteiisch*
  | *neutral.* — *neutral*
  to *judge* somebody | by his attitude to / towards … / on what he did. — *beurteilen*
  to judge somebody | objectively. / in an objective way.
- | to *hold* / to *have* | *a prejudice* against … } — *ein Vorurteil haben*

2.1.6. Überzeugt sein *(to be convinced)*

- The author is *convinced* that … — *überzeugt*
- He is | *sure* / *certain* | that … / about … } — *sicher*
- It is his *conviction* that … — *Überzeugung*
  He expresses his conviction that …

2.2. Die positive Meinung *(the positive opinion)*

2.2.1. Eine positive Meinung haben, billigen *(to approve)*

- to have a | *good* / *positive* / *favourable* / *high* | *opinion* of / about … } — *gute Meinung* / *positive Meinung* / *günstige Meinung* / *hohe Meinung*
  to *pass a favourable judgement on* … / to *take a positive view of* … } — *positiv beurteilen*

• to *approve of* sth	*billigen*
• to *agree* with sb / sth	*gleicher Meinung sein*
to *agree* on / about sth	*einverstanden sein*
to agree to (do) sth	
• to *accept* / to *approve* sth	*akzeptieren*
• to *suggest* / to *propose* — sth to sb / that ...	*vorschlagen*
to *make suggestions* about / on / how ...	*Vorschläge machen*
• to *advise* sb to do sth	*raten, beraten*
to *give advice* to sb	*Ratschläge geben*
to *give sb a piece of advice*	*jdm einen Rat geben*
to *recommend* — that ... / sb to do sth	*empfehlen*
to make a *recommendation* to sb that ...	*Empfehlung*
• to *praise* sb / sth for ...	*loben*
to *acknowledge* / to *recognize* — that ... / sb / sth to be ...	*anerkennen*
to *identify with* ...	*sich identifizieren mit*
to *sympathize* with ...	*sympathisieren*
international *solidarity*	*Solidarität*
to *show one's solidarity with* ...	*solidarisch sein mit*
to expresses one's *sympathy* for ...	*Mitgefühl*
to have a *liking* for ...	*Vorliebe*
• to show one's *respect* for ...	*Respekt*
• to express one's *satisfaction* at / with sth	*Zufriedenheit*

2.2.2. Sich einsetzen für *(to support)*

• to *be* (all) *for* ... / to *be in favour of* ...	*dafür sein*
• to *support* sb / sth	*unterstützen*
to *argue in support of* sth / *for* ...	*sich aussprechen für*
to *speak in favour of* ...	*sich äußern zugunsten*
to *take somebody's part*	*jds Partei ergreifen*
• to *fight for* ...	*kämpfen für*
• The author's social *commitment* shows *in the fact that* ...	*Engagement in der Tatsache, dass ...*
• to *defend* sb against / from ...	*verteidigen*

2.3. Die negative Meinung *(the negative opinion)*

2.3.1. Eine negative Meinung haben, missbilligen *(to disapprove)*

• to have a *bad* / a *negative* / an *unfavourable* / a *low* *opinion* of / about ...	*schlechte Meinung* / *negative Meinung* / *ungünstige Meinung* / *geringe Meinung*
to *pass an unfavourable judgement on ...* / to *take a negative view of ...*	*negativ beurteilen*
• The author *disapproves of ...*	*missbilligen*
• He *disagrees* with (the ideas of ...)	*anderer Meinung sein*
• The author does *not accept ...* / does *not approve ...*	*nicht akzeptieren*
• He *refuses* to do sth	*sich weigern*
• He *rejects* sth	*ablehnen*
The author does not *share* *somebody's opinion* of / about ... / the opinion according to which ...	*jds Meinung teilen*
The author expresses / shows his strong *dislike* of / for ...	*Abneigung*
his *aversion* to ...	*Aversion*
his *antipathy* to(wards) ...	*Antipathie*

2.3.2. Kritisieren, in Frage stellen *(to criticize, to question)*

• to *criticize* sb / sth for ...	*kritisieren*
to *express vehement criticism of ...*	*heftige Kritik äußern an*
to *call sth into question*	*etw. in Frage stellen*
He calls the traditional values into question.	
to *question sth*	*etw. in Frage stellen, bezweifeln*
He questions the truth of these statements.	
• to *doubt* sth / that ...	*bezweifeln*
He doubts the *necessity* of taking these measures.	*Notwendigkeit*
• to express *doubts* about sth	*Zweifel*

2.3.3. Vorwerfen, anklagen *(to reproach, to accuse)*

• to *reproach* sb for sth / for (not) doing sth / for (not) having done sth	*vorwerfen*
to express *reproach*	*Vorwurf*
• These reproaches are *unjustified.*	*ungerechtfertigt*
• to *blame* sb for ... / • to *accuse* sb of arrogance / of being arrogant	*anklagen, beschuldigen*

to *condemn* sb or sth	*verurteilen*
He condemns (the *passivity* of the onlookers).	*Passivität*

2.3.4. Sich aussprechen gegen *(to argue against)*

• to *be against sth*	*gegen etw. sein*
to *argue against* ...	*sich aussprechen gegen*
• to *oppose* sth	*sich widersetzen*
• to *contradict* sb / sth	*widersprechen*
• to *protest* about / against / at ...	*protestieren*
• the *protest* against ...	*Protest(e)*
• to *fight against* ...	*kämpfen gegen*
• a *fight* against ...	*Kampf*

2.3.5. Vorbehalte haben, sich distanzieren *(to have reservations)*

• to *have reservations* about ...	*Vorbehalte haben*
to *have misgivings* about ...	*Befürchtungen haben*
The author *dis(as)sociates himself* from ...	*sich distanzieren*
The author does not *identify with* ...	*sich identifizieren mit*

2.4. Weitere Ausdrücke *(further expressions)*

2.4.1. Erklären, angeben, mitteilen, behaupten *(to explain, to state, to inform, to maintain)*

• to *say* that ... • to *state* that ...	*feststellen*
This *statement* is not justified.	*Feststellung, Aussage*
• to *explain* sth / that ...	*erklären*
• to give an *explanation* for / of ...	*Erklärung*
• to *state* that ...	*erklären*
• to *give* / • to *state* the reasons why ...	*angeben, nennen*
• to *mention* sb / sth / that ...	*erwähnen*
• The author's statements are *correct.*	*richtig*
• *accurate.*	*genau*
incorrect.	*unrichtig*
inaccurate.	*ungenau*
• to *express* sth	*ausdrücken*
• to *point out* that ...	*hinweisen auf*
• to *inform* sb of / about ...	*mitteilen*
to *make sb understand*	*jdm begreiflich machen*
to *observe* that ... to *remark* that ...	*bemerken, sagen*

to make *remarks* (up)on ... to make *observations* about ...	*Bemerkung, Äußerung*
to *acknowledge* that ... to *admit* that ...	*zugeben, einräumen*
• to *maintain* that ...	*behaupten*
to *claim* to have done sth	*behaupten, vorgeben*
• to *pretend* to do sth	*behaupten, vorgeben*
The author pretends to know why young people take drugs.	

2.4.2. Schildern, darstellen, beschreiben, charakterisieren *(to depict, to show, to describe, to characterize)*

• to *show* sth to *represent* sth (as ...)	*darstellen*
He represents the peasants' life (as very hard).	
His *representation* of (rural life) conveys an impression of (peacefulness).	*Darstellung*
to *depict* sth	*schildern*
He depicts social life in Britain.	
to *portray* sth (as ...)	*schildern*
He portrays British society (as ...).	
to *paint a picture of* sth	*schildern*
• to *remind* (sb) *of* sth	*erinnern an*
He reminds (the reader) of the political events of 1992.	
• to *describe* sth	*beschreiben*
He describes the countryside (to the reader).	
• He gives a detailed *description* of (industrialized societies).	*Beschreibung*
• He describes the *characteristics* / • *features* of modern life.	*Kennzeichen, Merkmal*
• He gives the *typical traits* of sth	*besondere Eigenschaft*
• to *characterize* sb as ...	*charakterisieren*
The author characterizes this man as a *weak* person.	*schwach*
• The text is characterized by / • marked by the *shortness* of the sentences.	*Kürze*
the *length* of the sentences.	*Länge*

2.4.3. Berichten, erzählen, erwähnen; verschweigen *(to report, to tell, to mention; to conceal)*

• to *report* sth to *recount* sth	*berichten von*
to give an *account* of ... • a (newspaper) *report* on / of	*Bericht*
• In this text the author *speaks about* ... • In this lecture, the speaker *talks about* ...	*sprechen über*

• to *tell* sb (about) sth	*erzählen*
The author tells the reader (about) a story.	
to tell sb that ... / why, what, how ...	
to *relate* sth	*erzählen*
• to *mention* sth (to sb)	*erwähnen*
• to *add* sth	*hinzufügen*
to *allude to* ... / to *hint at* ...	*anspielen auf*
The author makes an *allusion* to ... / He gives *hints* about ...	*Anspielung*
He does *not* give *any exact details.*	*nichts Genaues*
• He does not *comment on* ...	*kommentieren*
to *conceal* sth from ...	*verschweigen*

2.4.4. Informieren; Beispiele / Einzelheiten nennen
(to inform; to give examples / details)

• to *inform* sb of / about sth / that ...	*informieren*
He informs the reader of / about the dangers of drugs.	
He informs him that it is necessary to take action now.	
• He gives *information* on / about ...	*Informationen, Auskunft*
• He gives *a piece of information.*	*eine Information*
• The information *is based on* facts.	*beruhen auf*
It is impossible to *verify* this information.	*nach-, überprüfen*
The *verification* of this information is impossible.	*Nach-, Überprüfung*
• to *give an example of* ...	*ein Beispiel nennen für*
• He gives some / several examples to prove his point ...	
• The author *quotes* a lot of *examples.*	*Beispiele anführen*
As an example he quotes (the government's attitude to ...)	*als Beispiel*
With this example he wants to prove ...	*mit diesem Beispiel*
• The author gives *details* which *concern* ...	*Einzelheit; betreffen*
• He presents details which *are related to* ...	*sich beziehen auf*
The author informs the reader *in detail* of / about ... / • He gives *detailed* information on / about ...	*detailliert*

2.4.5. Betonen, auf die Bedeutung hinweisen; appellieren
(to underline, to point out the importance; to appeal to)

• to *underline* / • to *stress* / to *emphasize* — sth / that ...	*betonen, unterstreichen*
to lay / • to put — *stress* on ... / *emphasis* on ...	*Betonung*
to *accentuate* sth	*betonen, akzentuieren*
• to *insist* *on ...*	*bestehen auf*
• to *insist* *that ...*	*darauf bestehen, dass ...*
to *attach* great *importance to ...*	*Bedeutung beimessen*
He attaches more importance to (freedom) than to (happiness).	
• to *draw* / to *call* — sb *attention* to ...	*Aufmerksamkeit lenken auf*
to make an *appeal* to sb (to do sth)	*Appell*
He makes an appeal to the reader (to take action).	
• to *appeal* to sb (for sth) / to sth	*appellieren*
He appeals to the reader (for support).	
He appeals to one's *common sense.*	*gesunder Menschenverstand*
• He appeals to emotions rather than to *reason.*	*Verstand, Vernunft*
• to *address* sb	*ansprechen*
The author addresses the reader directly.	

2.4.6. Zum Ausdruck bringen, zeigen, beweisen
(to express, to show, to prove)

• to *express* sth	*ausdrücken*
He expresses his tolerance of / towards foreigners.	
to *give expression to ...*	*zum Ausdruck bringen*
In this sentence he gives expression to his feelings.	
to *voice* sth	*zum Ausdruck bringen*
He voices his opinion.	
• to *reveal* sth	*enthüllen, verraten*
This sentence reveals the true character of ...	
• to *show* sth (to sb)	*zeigen*
The author shows his dislike of / for ...	
He shows us why he dislikes ...	
• His style *suggests* great sensitivity.	*schließen lassen auf*
• to *prove* sth (to sb)	*beweisen*
• He wants to prove (to the reader) that his attitude is right.	

to *provide* / to *furnish* / to *produce* — *proof* of ... / *evidence* of / for / that ...	*Beweise liefern*
to *have* — *proof* of ... / *evidence* of / for / that ...	*Beweise haben*
to *be* — *proof* of ... / *evidence* of / that ...	*Beweis sein*
• *a piece of evidence*	*ein Beweis*
• He quotes some examples *as proof of* ...	*als Beweis für*

2.4.7. Gedanken äußern *(to express thoughts)*

• to express / to utter / to voice — one's (personal) *ideas* on / about ...	*Idee, Gedanke, Vorstellung*
• to show the consequences which *result from* this idea	*sich ergeben aus*
• to point out the *advantages* and *disadvantages* of an idea	*Vorteil; Nachteil*
• This idea is illustrated with a number of examples.	
• the *main idea* / the *principal idea*	*Hauptgedanke*
the *essential* ideas	*wesentlich*
The main idea in this paragraph is ...	
• to *develop* an idea	*entwickeln*
He develops the idea of (liberty).	
to *take* an idea *up again* / to *come back to* an idea	*wieder aufnehmen*
He comes back to the idea developed in the first part.	
This word *evokes* the idea of (sadness). / The second paragraph *conveys* the idea of (loneliness).	*vermitteln*
to use — the *stereotype* of ... / *stereotyped ideas*	*Klischee* / *Klischeevorstellung*
• *the thought of* ...	*der Gedanke an*
• to expound one's *thoughts about* ...	*Gedanken über*
• to *think of* ...	*denken an*
• to *think* (deeply) *about* ... / to *reflect on / about* ...	*nachdenken über*
The *starting(-)point* of his *reflexions* is ...	*Ausgangspunkt; Überlegungen*

2.4.8. Eindrücke äußern, Gefühle äußern
(to voice impressions, to utter feelings)

- to give (sb) the *impression* of ... / that ... — *Eindruck*
- to have / to get the impression that ...
- to *create* / to *produce* an impression of (sadness) — *hervorrufen*
- to *impress* sb with ... — *beeindrucken*
- to express one's / to utter one's *feelings* / *emotions* — *Gefühle*
- He expresses a f*eeling of loneliness.* — *Gefühl der Einsamkeit*
- He expresses the *wish* to do sth. — *Wunsch*
- to *have a* great *feeling of* / to *be filled with* / to *feel* *joy* — *Gefühl der Freude empfinden*

2.4.9. Untersuchen; unterscheiden *(to examine; to distinguish)*

- to *examine* sth — *untersuchen,*
  He examines both aspects of the problem.
  to *study* sth — *sich befassen mit,*
  He studies (the different aspects of sth).
  to *analyse* sth — *analysieren*
  He analyses the recent situation in Britain.

- to do a

detailed	*examination* of ...	
close	*analysis* of ...	*genaue Untersuchung*
careful	*study* of ...	

  to *distinguish* between ... — *unterscheiden*
  The author distinguishes between what they say and do.
  to draw a *distinction* between ... — *Unterscheidung*
- to tell the *difference* between ... — *Unterschied*

2.4.10. Vergleichen, gegenüberstellen *(to compare, to contrast)*

- to *compare ... to / with ...* — *vergleichen mit*
  He compares life in Britain to / with life in other countries.
- to *make* / to *draw* *a comparison* between ... and ... — *einen Vergleich ziehen*
  to *establish a relationship* between ... and ... — *eine Beziehung herstellen*
- to *relate ... to / with ...* — *in Beziehung setzen mit*
  He relates the increase in crime to drug abuse.
  to *establish a connection* between ... and ... — *eine Verbindung herstellen*
- to *connect ... to / with ...* — *in Verbindung setzen mit*
  He connects smoking to cancer.

• to *contrast* two things	*gegenüberstellen*
He contrasts two different attitudes towards foreigners.	
• a *contrast* between ...	*Gegensatz, Kontrast*
to *be in contrast with ...*	*im Gegensatz stehen zu*
There is a contrast between the style and the contents.	
The style is in contrast with the contents of the text.	

2.4.11. Kommentieren, interpretieren *(to comment, to interpret)*

• to *comment on* sth	*kommentieren*
He comments on (the results of the survey).	
• to make a *comment* on / about ...	*Kommentar*
He makes a comment on the current situation in Britain.	
• to *interpret sth ...*	*interpretieren, deuten*
He interprets (the reasons for his behaviour).	
• to give a personal *interpretation* of sth	*Interpretation, Deutung*

2.4.12. Argumente / Einwände vorbringen *(to put forward arguments / objections)*

• The author *puts forward the thesis* that ...	*die These aufstellen*
The author's *theses* are ...	*Thesen*
• He *maintains* that ...	*behaupten*
• He *contradicts the statement* about ...	*der Behauptung widersprechen*
He illustrates his thesis with several examples.	
He quotes two examples in order to *support* his thesis.	*untermauern*
• He supports his thesis with two *arguments.*	*Argument*
To *substantiate* his view, he gives two arguments.	*begründen, belegen*
to *qualify one's statement*	*seine Behauptung einschränken*
He qualifies his statement by adding that ...	
to *give* / to *advance* | *arguments* | for sth / against sth	*Argumente vorbringen*
to *disprove* an argument	*widerlegen*
• to *reject* an argument	*zurückweisen*
• His arguments are *convincing.*	*überzeugend*
• *strong.*	*stark*
• *logical.*	*logisch*
• His arguments are rather *weak.*	*schwach*
• *illogical.*	*unlogisch*
• The author bases his *argumentation* on facts. / His *reasoning* is based on facts.	*Argumentation*
His argumentation is *partial.* / *partisan.*	*parteiisch*
impartial.	*unparteiisch*

• He is not *convinced* by these arguments.	*überzeugt*
• The author *argues* in a convincing way.	*argumentieren*
to *formulate a hypothesis*	*eine Hypothese aufstellen*
This *confirms* the author's *assumption.*	*bestätigen; Annahme*
It is impossible to *verify* this hypothesis.	*nach-, überprüfen*
• The author voices *objections* to ...	*Einwand*
He *makes objections* to ...	*Einwände erheben*
• He *comes to the conclusion that ...*	*zu dem Schluss kommen, dass ...*
• *From this he concludes that ...*	*Er folgert daraus, dass ...*

2.4.13. Gründe / Folgen nennen (to state reasons / consequences)

• the *reason* for (doing) sth / to do sth / why ... / that ...	*Grund*
to give reasons	
• to *enumerate* the reasons which explain sth	*aufzählen*
The reason for this is that ...	*der Grund dafür ist, dass ...*
• to show the *consequence* which results from ...	*Folge*
As a consequence of this ...	*als Folge davon*
The consequence of this is ...	*die Folge davon ist ...*
• *This leads to* (an increase in violence).	*dies führt zu ...*
This may *have* grave *consequences.*	*Folgen haben*
This *means* that ...	*bedeuten*

2.4.14. Sich etwas vorstellen *(to imagine sth)*

• to *imagine sth* / that ...	*sich etw. vorstellen*
He imagines a *future* without war.	*Zukunft*
He imagines that the future is *uncertain.*	*ungewiss*
• to *have clear ideas on / about* sth	*genaue Vorstellungen haben von*
He has clear ideas on / about (the problems to be solved).	
to *have a wrong idea of / about ...*	*eine falsche Vorstellung haben von*
He has a wrong idea about (young people).	
an *outlook* on life	*Sichtweise*
• His outlook on life is *optimistic.*	*optimistisch*
• *pessimistic.*	*pessimistisch*
to *take an idealistic view* of ...	*eine idealistische Sicht haben*
He takes an idealistic view of the world.	

2.4.15. Sich bewusst sein; berücksichtigen
(to be aware of; to take into consideration)

- to *be* | *aware* / *conscious* | of sth / that … — *sich bewusst sein*
- He is not aware of the *gravity* of the problem. — *Schwere*
- He is conscious that drugs *pose a problem* — *ein Problem darstellen*
- He knows that drug abuse *causes problems*. — *Probleme schaffen*
- to *take sth into consideration* / to *take account of sth*
- to *consider sth* — *etw. berücksichtigen*

  He does not | take (the drug problem) into consideration. / take account of (the drug problem). / consider (the drug problem).
- to *consider that …*
- to *take into consideration that …* — *berücksichtigen, dass …*

  One has to take into consideration that (to some problems there aren't any solutions).

2.4.16. Die Darstellungsweise des Autors werten
(to evaluate the author's way of presenting information)

- to *exaggerate* (sth) — *übertreiben*

  The author exaggerates greatly when he says that …
- an *exaggeration* — *Übertreibung*

  This passage *contains* an exaggeration. — *enthalten*
- to *generalize* (about sth) — *verallgemeinern*

  Saying that …, the author generalizes.

  He generalizes about (young people).
- a *generalization* — *Verallgemeinerung*

  This generalization cannot be justified.
- to *simplify* sth — *vereinfachen*

  Simplifying the problem is no solution for it.
- a *simplification* — *Vereinfachung*

  This is a great simplification of the problem.
- to *underestimate* sb / sth — *unterschätzen*

  The author underestimates (the dangers of drug abuse).
- to *overestimate* sb / sth — *überschätzen*

  He overestimates the possibilities the police have to combat crime.
- to *idealize* — *idealisieren*

  The author idealizes reality.

2.5. Die Absicht des Autors *(the author's intention)*

• It is the author's *intention* to do sth / that ...	*Absicht*
The author *intends* to ...	*beabsichtigen*
It is the author's *goal* to ...	
• The *purpose* / • The *aim* / The *objective* — of the text is ... / of the author is ...	*Ziel*
The author *pursues* *the goal* of ... / *the aim* to do / of doing sth	*das Ziel verfolgen*
• He tries to *achieve* / • *reach* — *his goals.* / *his aims.*	*seine Ziele erreichen*
• The author wants to *influence* the reader.	*beeinflussen*
He *exerts an influence* on ...	*einen Einfluss ausüben*
• *to want sb to do sth*	*wollen, dass ... jd etw. tut*
He wants the reader to form his own opinion of / about ...	
• He wants to *persuade* the reader to (buy the product).	*überreden*
He wants to *urge* the reader to (change his mind).	*drängen*
• He wants to *encourage* the reader to (act).	*ermutigen*
• *to make sb do sth*	*jdn veranlassen. etw. zu tun*
He wants to make the reader (think).	
to cause sb to do sth	*jdn veranlassen. etw. zu tun*
He tries to cause the reader to (adopt his opinion).	
• He wants to *draw* / *direct* *the* reader's *attention to* ...	*die Aufmerksamkeit lenken auf*
• He wants to *appeal* to the reader to ...	*appellieren*
He wants to *make* the reader *sensitive to* ... the immigrants' problems.	*sensibilisieren für*
• He wants to *tell* the reader *about* (his thoughts).	*mitteilen*
• to *make* him *understand* that ... / to *make* him *realize* that ...	*begreiflich machen*
• to *open the reader's eyes to* ...	*jdm die Augen öffnen für*
to *warn* the reader *of* an increase in crime.	*warnen vor*
• to *convince* the reader of sth / to do sth / that his position is right.	*überzeugen*
to *manipulate* the reader.	*manipulieren*
to *justify* (the government's latest initiatives).	*rechtfertigen*
• to *defend* (the immigrants) from / against ...	*verteidigen*
• to *evoke emotions* in / within the reader.	*Gefühle hervorrufen*
• to *shock* the reader.	*schocken*
• to *arouse* the reader's *interest*.	*Interesse wecken*
• to arouse the reader's *curiosity* about sth	*Neugier*
• to make him *curious* about sth by telling him that ...	*neugierig*
to arouse the reader's *sympathy*.	*Mitgefühl*
• It is difficult to *find out* the author's intentions.	*herausfinden*

• His intention to be *polemic* shows in ...	*polemisch*
• His intention to *satirize* society is obvious in the *use* of ...	*satirisch darstellen*; *Verwendung, Gebrauch*

3. DIE TEXTSORTEN *(the genres)* DER LITERARISCHE / FIKTIONALE TEXT *(the literary / fictional text)*

3.1. Der erzählende Text *(the narrative text)*

3.1.1. Allgemeines *(general terms)*

• the *novel*	*Roman*
the *autobiographical* novel	*autobiografisch*
• the *detective novel*	*Kriminalroman*
• the *science fiction novel*	*Sciencefictionroman*
• the *short story*	*Kurzgeschichte*
• the *detective story*	*Kriminalgeschichte*
• the *science fiction story*	*Sciencefictiongeschichte*
the *tale*	*Erzählung, Geschichte*
the *narrative*	*Erzählung, Bericht*
the *anecdote*	*Anekdote*
the *narrative* text	*erzählend*
the *novelist*	*Romanschriftsteller*
• the *author / writer*	*Schriftsteller*
interior monologue	*innerer Monolog*

3.1.2. Die Kriminalgeschichte *(the detective story)*

• to *commit* | *a crime*	*ein Verbrechen begehen*
• | a *murder*	*Mord*
• the *criminal*	*Verbrecher*
• the *murderer*	*Mörder*
The inspector | *conducts an investigation.*	*eine Untersuchung durchführen*
| *investigates* the murder.	*untersuchen*
• He is searching for the person who is *guilty* of the crime.	*schuldig*
He *conducts an interrogation.*	*ein Verhör durchführen*
• He *interrogates* | the *suspects.*	*verhören; Verdächtige*
| the people *concerned in / with* the crime.	*betroffen von*
He *verifies* the statements made by the suspects.	*überprüfen*
• One of the persons interrogated by the police must *lie.*	*lügen*
He formulates a *hypothesis* concerning ...	*Hypothese, Annahme*
The police are searching for *clues* to ... / about ...	*Indiz*
• The inspector *suspects* sb of | having committed the crime.	*verdächtigen*
| being involved in the murder.	

• He suspects an *innocent* man.	*unschuldig*
• His behaviour made the police *suspicious.*	*misstrauisch*
• He is a *suspicious*-looking individual.	*verdächtig*
He made himself suspicious.	
• There weren't any *(eye)witnesses.*	*(Augen)Zeuge*
• There is no *clear motive* for the murder.	*ein klares Motiv*
The police arrive on the *scene of the crime.*	*Tatort*
• The Inspector examines the room for *fingerprints.*	*Fingerabdrücke*
• The Inspector examines the *weapon* for *fingerprints.*	*Waffe*
• The Inspector examines the garden for *footprints.*	*Fußabdrücke*
• The Inspector examines *the victim.*	*das Opfer*
• The murderer is *arrested.*	*verhaften*
the *personality* of the criminal	*Persönlichkeit*
the *identity* of the murderer	*Identität*
• The story is told *from the point of view of* (a neighbour).	*aus der Sicht*
• The author arouses the reader's *curiosity.*	*Neugier*
• The author makes the reader *curious.*	*neugierig*

3.1.3. Die Sciencefictiongeschichte *(the science fiction story)*

A science fiction story is set in *the future.*	*Zukunft*
Science has *advanced* considerably.	*Fortschritte machen*
Man seeks to come into contact with other planets.	
It is the astronaut's mission to *explore* other planets.	*erforschen*
the *exploration* of the universe	*Erforschung*
He is searching for *alien* life-forms. / He is searching for *extraterrestrial* life(-forms).	*außerirdisch*
He encounters *aliens.* / *extraterrestrials.* / *extraterrestrial beings.*	*Außerirdische*
He does not find any *humans.* / *human beings.*	*menschliche Wesen*
They travel in a *spacecraft.*	*Raumschiff*
Man builds machines of extraordinary *power.*	*Kraft, Stärke*
He *has no power* to control his creation.	*machtlos, ohnmächtig sein*
He is *dependent on* robots.	*abhängig von*
They are *superior* to man.	*überlegen*
• They are *able* to control human beings.	*fähig*
Machines destroy the *relationship between human beings.*	*zwischenmenschliche Beziehungen*
This *involves* a great danger to *mankind.*	*mit sich bringen; Menschheit*
The author *anticipates* the future.	*vorausahnen, vorwegnehmen*

The *time traveller* uses a time machine to move *backward(s) / forward(s)* in time.	*Zeitreisender* *rückwärts; vorwärts*
Science fiction often contains *fantastical* elements.	*fantastisch*

3.1.4. Der Comic *(the comic strip)*

a *comic (book)*	*Comicheft*
a *comic strip*	*Comicgeschichte*
The comic strip contains *humorous* elements.	*humoristisch*
It deals with a subject in a humorous way.	
It presents reality in a *simplified* way.	*vereinfacht*
It is a caricature rather than a *true picture* of reality.	*genaues Abbild*
a *balloon*	*Sprechblase*
Big letters *suggest* sb is speaking at the top of his / her voice.	*hindeuten auf*
The author uses | *onomatopoeia*.	*Lautmalerei*
| *onomatopoeic* words.	*lautmalerisch*
The character's state of mind is reflected in the pictures.	

3.2. Das Theaterstück *(the play)*

3.2.1. Das Drama, die Tragödie *(the drama, the tragedy)*

3.2.1.1. Der Aufbau *(the structure)*

• the *play*	*Theaterstück*
• the *tragedy*	*Tragödie*
• the *drama*	*Drama*
• The *action* takes place (in London).	*Handlung*
The action is set in (a hotel).	
The *starting(-)point* of / for the action is ...	*Ausgangspunkt*
There are several *subplots* to the *main plot*.	*Neben-; Haupthandlung*
• The first scene | gives the *setting* of / for the action.	*Rahmen*
• | *introduces* the situation.	*einführen*
• The *conflict* develops in several stages.	*Konflikt*
• The typical plot of a five-act play *consists of*	*bestehen aus*
the *rising action* / the *complication* and	*steigende Handlung*
the *falling action*.	*fallende Handlung*
The first scene of the first act is the *exposition*.	*Exposition*
The exposition | gives information on / about ...	
| informs us of / about ...	
| is an introduction to the action.	
| indicates the time, the place and	
• *the circumstances* of the action.	*die Umstände*
• the rule of the three *unities*	*Einheit*

the unity of action, time and place	
The plot has unity of action.	
• The *playwright* respects this rule.	*Bühnenschriftsteller*
• In the second scene of the first act the *intrigue* begins to *develop*.	*Intrige; sich anbahnen*
In Act 1, Scene 2 the conflict *builds up*.	*sich anbahnen*
• The conflict reaches its *climax* in Scene 1, Act 3.	*Höhepunkt*
• The *crisis* is / • The *turning(-)point* comes — in the fourth scene of Act 5.	*Wendepunkt*
The climax can be identical with the turning(-)point.	
In the middle of the play, there is a *reversal*.	*plötzlicher Umschwung*
• The final scene represents the *denouement*.	*Lösung (Theater)*
catastrophe.	*Katastrophe*
• In the last scene the conflict *is solved*.	*sich lösen*
• The play has a happy *ending*. / tragic ending.	*Ende (Theater)*

3.2.1.2. Die Handlung *(the action)*

• The action is *improbable*.	*unwahrscheinlich*
• is *unbelievable*. / • is *implausible*.	*unglaubhaft*
• lacks *plausibility*.	*Glaubhaftigkeit*
does not *reflect* real life.	*widerspiegeln*
• This is one of the *central* scenes of the play.	*zentral*
• This scene is important for the *development of the action*.	*Handlungsverlauf*
The action *progresses* fast.	*voranschreiten*
This scene *accelerates* the action.	*beschleunigen*
• This scene contains a *flashback*.	*Rückblende*
The scene is full of *retarding* elements.	*verzögern*
The development of the action / progress of the plot is *slowed down*.	*verlangsamen*
• The action is *interrupted* by ...	*unterbrechen*
In this scene, the action comes to a *standstill*. / is brought to a *halt*.	*Stillstand*
The tragic ending / The catastrophe is *delayed*.	*hinauszögern*
This scene also contains some *narrative* passages.	*erzählend*

3.2.1.3. Die Personen *(the characters)*

• *the stage*	*die Bühne*
In this scene the main characters *are on stage*.	*auftreten, auf der Bühne sein*

•	the *main* / *chief* *character*; the *protagonist*	*Hauptperson*
	the *antagonist*	*Gegenspieler*
	the *hero*	*Held*
	the *heroine*	*Heldin*
	The hero *leaves the stage.*	*die Bühne verlassen*
	the protagonist's *entry*	*Auftritt, Auftreten*
	the protagonist's *exit*	*Abtritt, Abtreten*
	This scene contains *descriptive* passages.	*beschreibend*
•	In this scene the playwright *characterizes* the antagonist.	*charakterisieren*
	He gives a *characterization* of the antagonist.	*Personenbeschreibung*
•	The author gives a detailed description of the chief character's *outward appearance.*	*äußere Erscheinung*
	He describes the character's *gestures.*	*Geste*
•	He shows the hero's *motives* for ...	*Motiv*
• •	He shows the hero's *feelings.* / *emotions.*	*Gefühl*
	He presents the character's *social background.*	*Milieu*
•	The author portrays *believable* characters.	*glaubhaft*
	The author's *portrayal* of this character is believable.	*Darstellung*
•	The *actor's* portrayal of this character is believable.	*Schauspieler*
•	The *actress* portrays the heroine in a believable way.	*Schauspielerin*
•	This portrait *gives a* realistic *impression.*	*einen Eindruck vermitteln*
•	The characters are described *realistically.*	*realistisch* (Adv.)
•	The characters in this play are mere *types.*	*Typen*
•	The author gives only a *vague* description of	*verschwommen*
•	the hero's *traits of character.*	*Charakterzug*
	The characters are not really *involved in* the action.	*verwickelt in*
	The main character *represents* the author.	*darstellen*
	The main character is the *mouthpiece* of the author.	*Sprachrohr*

3.2.1.4. Der Konflikt *(the conflict)*

•	the *conflict* between *opposing* desires within the character himself	*Konflikt; gegensätzlich*
	This scene shows the conflict between (love) and (duty).	
	The protagonist is in conflict with his own feelings.	
•	the conflict between the hero and *fate*	*Schicksal*
•	the conflict between the character and his *environment*	*Umgebung*
	The conflict results from ...	

3.2.1.5. Der Dialog *(the dialogue)*

• In this scene there is a *dialogue* between ... and ...	*Dialog*
• The dialogue *deals with* ...	*handeln von*
The *subject* of the dialogue is ...	*Thema*
The hero does not listen to his *interlocutor*.	*Gesprächspartner*
• He does not listen to his interlocutor's *answer.* / *reply.*	*Antwort*
to *react* to sb / sth / to *respond*	*reagieren*
He does not react to (his interlocutor's replies).	
He says something, but his interlocutor does not respond.	
• a *reaction* / a *response*	*Reaktion*
• There is a *misunderstanding* between ... and ...	*Missverständnis*
• The tone of his reply is *ironical.*	*ironisch*
sarcastic.	*sarkastisch*
• This dialogue *is* mainly *characterized by* irony.	*bestimmt sein von*
• This scene consists of / contains a *monologue.*	*Monolog*
a *soliloquy.*	*Selbstgespräch*
• In this soliloquy, the protagonist *reveals* his motives.	*enthüllen*
• In this monologue, the hero *addresses*	*ansprechen*
• the *audience.*	*Publikum, Zuschauer*

3.2.1.6. Die Regieanweisungen *(the stage directions)*

The *stage directions* give information on / about ...	*Regieanweisungen*
• This information is about	
• the actor / the actress who *plays the role* of ...	*die Rolle spielen*
the time and place of the action.	

3.2.2. Die Komödie *(the comedy)*

3.2.2.1. Die verschiedenen Arten der Komik *(the different forms of the comic)*

• the *comedy*	*die Komödie*
The author uses different forms of *the comic.*	*Komik*
The comic effect *is based on* the fact that ...	*beruhen auf*
is *produced* by	*hervorrufen*
• The characters' behaviour is *ridiculous.*	*lächerlich*
• *strange.*	*merkwürdig*
• *bizarre.*	*wunderlich*
exaggerated.	*übertrieben*

The character uses language which does not	
correspond to / with | his *social status.*	*soziale Stellung*
| his *intellectual level.*	*geistiges Niveau*
• | his *job/profession.*	*Beruf/akademischer Beruf*
What is *comical* about the style is that one character	*komisch, lustig*
• *imitates* the language of another character.	*imitieren*
• The comic elements in this scene	
• are the | *misunderstandings.*	*Missverständnis*
• | *confusions.*	*Verwechslung*

3.2.2.2. Die Elemente der Komik (the elements of the comic)

• | This scene | contains | several *comic(al)* elements.	*komisch*
• | The dialogue | *includes* | several *funny* details	*beinhalten; lustig*
• The fact that ... *has a comic effect.*	*... wirkt komisch*
• The comic effect *results from* the fact that the audience has / have more information than the hero.	*sich ergeben aus*
The comic *consists in* the fact that the hero is in an	*bestehen in*
• *extreme* situation.	*extrem*
He *makes a fool of himself.*	*sich lächerlich machen*
He *makes* others *look foolish.*	*jdn lächerlich machen*
This character's manner of speaking	
provokes laughter.	*Gelächter hervorrufen*
The audience *laugh about / at ...*	*lachen über*
What is also comic(al) in this scene is ...	
Another comic(al) element is ...	
The dialogue is amusing because of the contrast between ...	
It is the contrast between ... that makes the dialogue comical.	

This scene contains a dialogue between two *deaf persons.*	*Tauber*
The people taking part in the conversation do not listen to each other.	
The conversation between these people is *absurd.*	*absurd*
the *absurdity* of the conversation	*Absurdität*
The answers show a lack of *logic.*	*Logik*
The style is not *appropriate for / to* a realistic dialogue.	*passen zu*
The style is rather *affected.*	*gekünstelt*
The conversation consists mainly of *banalities.*	*Banalität*
The characters make only *banal* remarks.	*banal*
The dialogue *is* entirely *composed of*	*sich zusammensetzen aus*
| *commonplaces.*	*Gemeinplatz*
| *trivial* remarks.	*trivial*
• The pun is based on the use of *ambiguous* words.	*zwei-, mehrdeutig*
• The pun is based on the *ambiguity* of these expressions.	*Zwei-, Mehrdeutigkeit*
This leads to *numerous* misunderstandings.	*zahlreich*

3.2.3. Der Sketch *(the sketch)*

The text presents	
• a *satire* on (the *consumer society*).	*Satire; Konsumgesellschaft*
• a *caricature* of (the typical consumer).	*Karikatur*
• a *parody* of (*advertising language*).	*Parodie; Werbesprache*
The author *parodies* (the language used in advertisements).	*parodieren*
• The characters are in an *absurd* situation.	*absurd*
• The situation is not *realistic*.	*realistisch*
The author *takes* the situation *to extremes*.	*bis zum Äußersten treiben*
• The conversation appears / seems (to be) illogical. / absurd.	
What the character says is completely *incoherent*.	*unzusammenhängend*
• The satirical aspect of the sketch *shows* mainly	*sich zeigen*
• in the *criticism of* ... / in somebody's exaggerated behaviour.	*Kritik an*
• It's the author's aim to *make us laugh* (at / about...).	*jmd zum Lachen bringen*
• But he also wants to draw our attention to behaviour that may be criticized.	
• The author wants to *make fun of* (advertising language).	*sich lustig machen über*

3.3. Das Gedicht *(the poem)*

3.3.1. Die Struktur des Gedichts *(the form of the poem)*

3.3.1.1. Die Strophe *(the stanza, the verse)*

• to analyse the *form* / *structure* *of the poem*	*Form des Gedichts*
• The poem *comprises* / *is composed of* / *consists of* / *has* four *stanzas*.	*umfassen; Strophe*
four *verses*.	*bestehen aus; Strophe*
• The first stanza comprises 5 *lines*.	*Vers, Zeile*
The first two stanzas consist of 5 lines.	
The stanzas have between 2 and 10 lines.	
The poem consists of 2 *tercets*.	*Dreizeiler*
The poem consists of 3 *quatrains* and	*Vierzeiler*
a *rhyming couplet*.	*Reimpaar*
Therefore it is a (Shakespearean) *sonnet*.	*Sonett*
• In the second stanza the *poet* expresses his feelings.	*Dichter*
• The structure / form of the poem is *regular*.	*regelmäßig*
irregular.	*unregelmäßig*
The first stanza has the same *syntactic structure* as the second stanza.	*syntaktische Struktur*

There is | *(a) correspondence* | between the two stanzas.	*Entsprechung*
| *parallelism* |	*Parallelismus*
• These two stanzas *belong together.*	*zusammengehören*
• The *sentence structure* is rather | *complex.*	*Satzbau; kompliziert*
• | *simple.*	*einfach*
There is a *break* | between the second and the third stanza.	*Bruch*
| in the syntactic structure.	
The third stanza has one more line than the first two stanzas.	
• The second stanza *is different* from the first.	*sich unterscheiden*
• There is a *difference* between the first and the second stanza.	*Unterschied*
One single sentence *constitutes* the final stanza.	*bilden*
• The poem *is not divided into* stanzas.	*eingeteilt sein in*
The poem can be divided into three parts	
• which are *equal* in length.	*gleich*
• The three parts of the poem are *unequal* in length.	*ungleich*
There is a contrast between the beginning and end.	

3.3.1.2. Der Vers *(the line, the verse)*

• an | *accented* | *syllable*	*eine betonte Silbe*
• | *stressed* |	
• an | *unaccented* | *syllable*	*eine unbetonte Silbe*
• | *unstressed* |	
The lines | have ten syllables.	
• | have five *iambic feet.*	*jambische Versfüße*
• | are iambic *pentameter(s).*	*Pentameter*
The lines | have twelve syllables.	
| have six iambic feet.	
| are iambic *hexameter.*	*Hexameter*
• The *length of the lines* is different.	*Zeilenlänge*
The lines have between 2 and 18 syllables.	
• The last lines of each stanza are | *identical.*	*identisch,*
• | *the same.*	*gleich*
• | *In line* 5 | the poet describes ...	*in Zeile*
• | *In* (the) *lines* 7 and 8 |	*in den Zeilen*
• Line 10 *deals with* ...	*handeln von*
The lines are composed of small *syntactic units.*	*syntaktische Einheit*
The third line is divided into 2 equal parts.	
The *caesura* after the word "..." stresses ...	*Zäsur*
The word "..." *is given prominence*	*... wird hervorgehoben*
by being placed at the beginning of the line.	
• The word "..." is *repeated* at the beginning of each stanza.	*wiederholen*
• The *repetition* of this word	*Wiederholung*
creates an impression of *monotony.*	*Monotonie*

In the second stanza there is an example of *enjamb(e)ment.*	*Enjambement, Zeilensprung*
Enjamb(e)ment occurs with the first and the second stanza.	*Strophensprung*
The syntactic element which appears at the beginning of the following line is given prominence.	
There is no *punctuation.*	*Zeichensetzung*
• There are no *punctuation marks.*	*Satzzeichen*
The *absence* of punctuation marks sometimes leads to difficulty in understanding the poem.	*Fehlen*

3.3.1.3. Der Reim *(the rhyme)*

• The *rhyme scheme* is aa bb cc.	*Reimschema*
• The lines *rhyme* aa bb cc.	*sich reimen*
• "Fear" rhymes with "here".	
The words "fear" and "bear" do not rhyme.	
• In the first stanza the rhyme scheme is | *regular.*	*regelmäßig*
• | *irregular.*	*unregelmäßig*
In the third stanza the rhyme is the same	
• as in the | *preceding* | stanzas.	*vorhergehend*
• | *following* |	*folgend*
The regular rhyme scheme and the equal length of the lines convey an impression of monotony.	

3.3.2. Detailanalyse des Gedichts *(detailed analysis of the poem)*

3.3.2.1. Allgemeines *(general remarks)*

• The *subject* of the poem is ...	*Thema*
The poet | *depicts* (the beauty of nature).	*schildern*
• | *describes* (an *imaginary* world).	*beschreiben; erdacht*
• | *creates* (an imaginary landscape).	*erschaffen*
• | *expresses* (his state of mind).	*ausdrücken*
• | *develops* the idea of (beauty).	*entwickeln*
• The *motif* of (sadness) *is taken up again* in the 3rd stanza.	*Motiv; wieder aufnehmen*
In the course of the poem, the *intensity* of this feeling becomes greater and greater.	*Intensität*
The "I" of the poem is the lyric speaker.	*das poetische Ich*
The voice we listen to in the poem	
• | is the voice of an *individual.*	*Individuum*
| is not identical with the poet's voice.	

The poet *expresses himself* in an indirect way.	*sich ausdrücken*
The poet does not give his opinion directly.	
The poet's *message* to the reader is that ...	*Botschaft*
The poet *conveys* a message to the reader.	*übermitteln*

3.3.2.2. Die Stilmittel *(the stylistic devices)*

The poet uses several *stylistic devices.* / *stylistic means.*	*Stilmittel*
The most important stylistic device in this poem is ...	
With this stylistic means he wants to / These stylistic means — express ... / underline ...	
The poet uses several *comparisons.*	*Vergleich*
The comparisons *refer to* ...	*sich beziehen auf*
to *be compared to* ...	*verglichen werden mit*
(Death) is compared to (sleep).	

The author uses *figurative language.*	*bildhafte Sprache*
The language is rich in *images.*	*(sprachliches) Bild*
In the first stanza there are several images.	
The first stanza contains several images.	

This image *conveys* the idea of (loneliness)	*vermitteln*
This image *suggests* a feeling of (loneliness).	*andeuten*
These are very *poetic(al)* images.	*poetisch*
symbolic	*symbolisch*
traditional	*traditionell*
vivid	*lebendig, anschaulich*
vague	*vage, verschwommen*
rather *banal*	*banal*
trivial	*trivial*

These images refer to / are related to (the sea and the sky).	
The images *are taken from* (reality).	*stammen aus*
The images *belong to* the *field* of (music).	*gehören zu; Bereich*

The images have *symbolic meaning.*	*symbolische Bedeutung*
The images have to be *taken as a symbol.*	*als Symbol auffassen*
The symbolic meaning of this image is difficult to understand.	

(The rose) is a *symbol of* (love).	*Symbol für*
(The rose) *symbolizes* (love).	*symbolisieren*
to *stand for* sth	*stehen für*
White stands for purity.	

• Line 6 contains | a *metaphor*.	*Metapher*
| a *metaphorical* expression.	*metaphorisch*
The metaphor | expresses ...	
| suggests ...	
The poet employs several | *figures of speech*.	*Redefiguren*
| *rhetorical figures*.	*rhetorische Figuren*
The beginning of each stanza is *marked* by	*kennzeichnen*
• the *repetition* of the same words.	*Wiederholung*
The repetition of the word "..." underlines ...	
• At the beginning of each stanza, the poet *repeats* the same words.	*wiederholen*
• He *takes* the same words *up again* at the beginning of each stanza.	*wieder aufnehmen*
In the 2nd stanza | there is an example of *parallelism*.	*Parallelismus*
• | there is a *parallel* in sentence structure.	*Parallele*
• The sentences have a *parallel* structure.	*parallel*
• In the 2nd stanza there is a *contrast* between the words ...	*Gegensatz, Kontrast*
The poet *contrasts ... with ...*	*etw. gegenüberstellen*
In the 2nd stanza, | there is an *antithesis*.	*Antithese*
| there are several *antitheses*.	*Antithesen*
• This sentence contains an *enumeration*.	*Aufzählung*
In this enumeration, there is an *increase* in intensity.	*Steigerung*
• The poet *enumerates ...*	*aufzählen*
In the 3rd stanza the poet uses *personification*.	*Personifizierung*
In the 3rd stanza, (melancholy) is *personified*.	*personifizieren*
The 1st stanza begins with an *exclamation*.	*Ausruf*
• In line 10 the poet uses a *rhetorical question*.	*rhetorische Frage*
• Line 12 contains an *allusion to ...*	*Anspielung auf*
The poet *alludes to ...*	*anspielen auf*
• In line 10 one can find a *paraphrase* of ...	*Umschreibung*
The poet uses a paraphrase *in reference to* (death).	*im Hinblick auf*
In this poem, ... is *paraphrased*.	*umschreiben*
The last two stanzas present several examples of *anaphora* which emphasize the statement.	*Anapher*

• In reference to (death) the poet uses a *euphemism*.	*Euphemismus*
The poet employs a *euphemistic* term for (death).	*euphemistisch*
Instead of the verb "to die" he uses the euphemistic expression "to pass away".	
Instead of using *the proper word* "…",	*das eigentliche Wort*
• which the reader might *find embarrassing*	*als peinlich empfinden*
the poet uses a less direct expression.	
• The stanzas 2 and 3 contain several *puns.* / *plays on words.*	*Wortspiel*
The poet *plays (up)on words.*	*mit Worten spielen*

3.3.2.3. Der Stil *(the style)*

• to analyse the *style* of a poem	*Stil*
• *As far as* the style *is concerned* / • *With regard to* the style — one can say …	*was … betrifft*
• The poem is written in *simple* language.	*einfach*
• *abstract*	*abstrakt*
harmonious	*harmonisch*
The poem is written in a *vivid* style.	*lebendig*
in an *elaborate*	*kunstvoll, ausgefeilt*
in a *ornate*	*überladen*
in a *pompous*	*schwülstig*
• The style is *characterized* by the use of many nouns.	*kennzeichnen*
• The use of many nouns is *characteristic of* the style.	*charakteristisch für*
• The great number of adjectives is *typical of* the style.	*typisch für*
It is the verbs that *predominate* in the poem.	*vorherrschen*
• Most of these verbs have a negative *meaning*.	*Bedeutung*
The poet uses simple words.	
• He employs mainly *concrete* words.	*konkret*
• *abstract* terms.	*abstrakt*
• *vague* expressions.	*vage, verschwommen*
• *ambiguous* words.	*doppel-, mehrdeutig*
affected expressions.	*gekünstelt*
The poet uses different *speech levels.* / *levels of speech.*	*Sprachebene*
• *literary* language	*literarisch*
• *formal*	*gehoben, formell*
• *informal* speech	*familiär, informell*
• *colloquial*	*umgangssprachlich*
• He employs *slang* (words, expressions).	*Slang*
• Many words belong to *everyday language*.	*Alltagssprache*

• A humorous effect results from this *combination.*	*Verbindung*
• The word "..." *suggests* ...	*denken lassen an*
• There is a close relationship between | the *contents* | and the form.	*Inhalt*
| *the content* |	*Gehalt*
The form *corresponds with / to* the contents.	*entsprechen*
There is (a) *correspondence* between the contents and the form.	*Übereinstimmung*

3.3.2.4. Der Rhythmus und der Klang *(the rhythm and the sounds in a poem)*

• The poem has | a *regular* | *rhythm.*	*gleichmäßig; Rhythmus*
• | an *irregular* |	*ungleichmäßig*
The rhythm is | *light.*	*leicht*
| *flowing.*	*fließend*
| *lively.*	*lebhaft*
• | *monotonous.*	*monoton*
| *jerky.*	*abgehackt*
• In the final stanza the rhythm | *becomes faster.* / *accelerates.*	*schneller werden*
The rhythm conveys the idea of *movement.*	*Bewegung*
• The rhythm underlines the impression of *joy.*	*Freude*
• The music gives the impression of *sadness.*	*Traurigkeit*
• It creates an atmosphere of *melancholy.*	*Melancholie*
The language is very *melodious.*	*wohlklingend*
The musical character of the poem shows above all in	
| the *frequent* use of certain *speech sounds.*	*häufig; Laut*
• | the *abundance* of *vowels.*	*Fülle; Vokal*
• | the *predominance* of *consonants.*	*Vorherrschen; Konsonant*
| *Dark* vowels | *predominate.*	*dunkel; dominieren*
| *Light* vowels |	*hell*
As a result, the general *mood* of the final part	*Stimmung*
| is *gloomy.*	*dunkel, düster*
• | is *cheerful.*	*fröhlich*
Line 10 contains | an example of *onomatopoeia.*	*Lautmalerei*
| *onomatopoeic* expressions.	*lautmalerisch*
The *effects* produced by the speech sounds give the poem its particular poetic character.	*Wirkung*

3.4. Das Lied *(the song)*

• This is a *poetic(al)* song.	*poetisch*
The song | is *critical of society.*	*sozialkritisch*
| contains *social criticism.*	*Sozialkritik*
• It is a *folk(-)song.*	*Volkslied*

The song is sung | by ...	
interpreted	*interpretiert*
• The *singer* is ...	*Interpret(in), Sänger(in)*
The *songwriter* | is ...	*Autor und Komponist*
composer	*Komponist*
• *... wrote the lyrics and the music*	*Text und Musik schreiben*
• The structure of the song is *regular.*	*regelmäßig*
• The stanzas are *irregular.*	*unregelmäßig*
• The song consists of four *verses.*	*Strophe*
• The 2nd verse is followed by a *refrain.*	*Refrain*
• It is the *function* of the refrain to ...	*Funktion*
• The refrain *expresses* a certain feeling.	*ausdrücken*
• There is a contrast between the *contents* of the verses	*Inhalt*
• and the refrain.	
• The verses contain four *lines.*	*Zeile*
• The length of the last *verse is different* from	*sich unterscheiden*
• the length of the other verses.	
• The song can be *divided* into four parts.	*unterteilen*
Each part *comprises* two verses.	*umfassen*
• The lines have between 5 and 8 *syllables.*	*Silben*
• The lines *rhyme* ab ab.	*sich reimen*
• The *rhyme scheme* is ab ab.	*Reimschema*
• The song *deals with* ...	*handeln von*
• The *theme* of the song is ...	*Thema*
• *The second verse* | *says* that ...	*es heißt im zweiten Vers*
• *describes* ...	*beschreiben*
• The singer addresses the | *listeners.*	*Zuhörer*
• *audience.*	*Publikum*
The lyrics and the music *are in harmony.*	*zueinander passen*
The music *goes (together) well with* the words.	*passen zu*
• The *tune* is simple.	*Melodie*
The music has a *calming* effect.	*beruhigen*
• The music is | *soft.*	*leise*
• *melancholy.* / *melancholic.*	*schwermütig*
• *sad.*	*traurig*
• *cheerful.*	*fröhlich*
rhythmic.	*rhythmisch*
• *loud.*	*laut*
• The rhythm is | *slow.*	*langsam*
• *fast.*	*schnell*
• *monotonous.*	*monoton*

• In the third verse the rhythm | *becomes faster.* / *accelerates.*	*schneller werden*
• The *change* in the rhythm *means* (that) ...	*Wechsel; bedeuten*
• This change *underlines* (that) ...	*unterstreichen*
• The singer's *voice* is sweet.	*Stimme*
• The singer's voice sounds *aggressive.*	*aggressiv*
• He / She interprets the song in a *sentimental* way.	*sentimental*
• The *musical instruments* are ...	*Musikinstrument*
• The singer is *accompanied on* | the *guitar.*	*begleiten auf; Gitarre*
• | the *piano.*	*Klavier*
| the *accordion.*	*Akkordeon*
• | the *flute.*	*Flöte*
• | the *violin.*	*Geige*
| *percussion.*	*Schlagzeug*
• He / She is accompanied by an *orchestra.*	*Orchester*
The guitar *accompaniment* underlines the melancholy character of the words.	*Begleitung*

3.5. Die Fabel *(the fable)*

(A fable can be written in prose or verse.)

• The *(beast) fable* has two parts:	*(Tier)Fabel*
• It consists of the story and the *moral.*	*Moral*
The moral is usually stated at the end of the fable.	
The last two lines are the moral.	
The first part of the text contains the action.	
• The text *combines* narrative (parts) and dialogue.	*verbinden*
Narrative parts *alternate* with dialogue.	*sich abwechseln*
• The narrative part shows the different *stages* of development of the action.	*Stufe*
• The lines 3 to 6 are the *exposition.*	*Einleitung*
• They *introduce* the reader to the situation.	*einführen*
In the exposition, the characters are introduced.	
• The lines give an *introduction* to the situation.	*Einführung*
The *protagonists* | are animals / beasts. / are plants.	*Protagonist*
• The action | takes place | in the *real* world.	*wirklich*
• | is set | in an *imaginary* place.	*ausgedacht*
• The lines 7 to 26 contain a dialogue between the *main characters.*	*Hauptfigur*

• The dialogue reveals the protagonists' *points of view.* / *viewpoints.*	*Standpunkt*
• The dialogue reveals the protagonists' *perspectives.*	*Blickwinkel*
• The lines 23 ff are the *dramatic* part of the fable.	*dramatisch*
• The lines 27 to 29 present the tragic *denouement.*	*Ausgang*
• The *ending* is tragic.	*Ende*
• The subject of the fable *concerns* ...	*betreffen*
• The fable is about *human* existence.	*menschlich*
• The animals talk and act like *human beings.*	*Mensch*
• The beasts *behave* like people.	*sich verhalten*
• The plants show human *behaviour.*	*Verhalten*
• The animals *stand for* human beings.	*stehen für*
The animals *represent* human beings.	*darstellen*
Their behaviour *illustrates* certain attitudes.	*verdeutlichen*
The author uses animals to *expose*	*entlarven*
the *excesses* of human behaviour.	*Auswüchse*
The moral is *exemplified* in the fable.	*exemplarisch darstellen*
• The moral can be *applied to* human society.	*übertragen auf*
• In the moral, the author criticizes the *faults* of / in ... / *flaws* in ...	*Fehler*
The moral is ...	
• The moral of the fable says that ...	
• In the moral the author *appeals to* the reader.	*appellieren an*
• He *addresses* the reader indirectly.	*ansprechen*
• The moral is *ironic(al)*: the author says	*ironisch*
• the *opposite* of what he really thinks.	*Gegenteil*
The ironic(al) character of the moral becomes apparent in the fact that ...	
• The truth is not stated / expressed *directly.*	*direkt*
The truth is not stated / expressed *explicitly.*	*klar und deutlich*
• The truth is stated *indirectly.*	*indirekt*
The truth is stated *implicitly.*	*implizit*
• The fable can be *interpreted* in several ways.	*interpretieren*

4. DIE TEXTSORTEN *(the genres)* DER NICHT-LITERARISCHE / NICHT-FIKTIONALE TEXT *(the non-literary / non-fictional text)*

4.1. Der Zeitungsartikel *(the newspaper article)*

• The article is taken from a *daily (paper).*	*Tageszeitung*
• The article is taken from a *weekly (paper).*	*Wochenzeitung*
• The article is taken from a *magazine.*	*Zeitschrift*
The article is taken from a *monthly (magazine).*	*Monatszeitschrift*
The article is taken from a *women's magazine.*	*Frauenzeitschrift*
• The article is taken from a *quality paper.*	*seriöses Blatt*
• The article is taken from a *popular paper.*	*Sensationsblatt*
The article is taken from a *scandal sheet.*	*Skandalblatt*
• The article is taken from a *local paper.*	*Lokalblatt*
• The *journalist* / The *correspondent* wrote / *edited* an article about ...	*Journalist*
	Korrespondent; redigieren
The *banner headline* makes people curious to read the paper.	*Balkenüberschrift*
• an eye-catching *headline*	*Schlagzeile*
The headline *is printed in large letters.*	*... ist fettgedruckt*
It *catches the* reader's *eye.*	*ins Auge springen*
The photo is on the *(front) cover.*	*Titelblatt*
• The article is printed on *the front page.*	*die erste Seite*
The article is in the literary *section.*	*Rubrik*
The article belongs to the column "*Miscellaneous*".	*„Vermischtes“*
• The text is a *letter to the editor.*	*Leserbrief*
• The text is an *advertisement.*	*Anzeige*
The text is an *ad(vert).*	*Anzeige* (ugs.)
The left *column* presents the facts.	*Spalte*
The right *column* contains the journalist's comment.	
• This newspaper article gives information on / about ...	
This newspaper article is an *analysis* of ...	*Analyse*
• The author presents information in an *objective* way.	*objektiv*
The author presents information objectively.	
• The journalist gives only *facts.*	*Tatsachen*
• The reporter informs the reader objectively of / about ...	
• The journalist *reports* the facts objectively.	*berichten*
• The journalist *reports on* the events objectively.	*berichten über*

• He does not *give his own opinion.*	*Stellung beziehen*
state his point of view.	*seinen Standpunkt darstellen*
The reporter's *source of information* is ...	*Informationsquelle*
• His information is *subjective.*	*subjektiv*
lacks *objectivity.*	*Objektivität*
is *(un)reliable.*	*(un)zuverlässig*
He does not reveal the identity of his *informant.*	*Informant*
His informant does not seem (to be) reliable.	
• The author is *prejudiced* against / in favour of sb.	*voreingenommen*
presents the facts in a *tendentious* way.	*tendenziös*
• The *news is* presented in a sensational way.	*die Nachrichten sind ...*
• The reporter uses terms which are intended to *create a sensation.*	*Aufsehen erregen*
• The presentation of the article *appeals to* the reader's	*ansprechen*
taste for sensations.	*Sensationslust*
Sensationalism is typical of the popular press.	*Effekthascherei*
• A *characteristic* of good journalistic style is ... / • A *typical feature* of this newspaper is ...	*Kennzeichen*
• The style of this article is *characterized* by ... / • is *marked* by ...	*kennzeichnen*
• The journalist *comments on ...*	*kommentieren*
makes comments on ...	*Bemerkungen machen*
The comment contains facts as well as the journalist's point of view on ...	
• The *commentator* expresses his personal opinion on / of / about ...	*Kommentator*
• The aggressive tone of the comment *shows* in the fact that ...	*sich zeigen*
The *editorial* / *leading article* offers an analysis of ...	*Leitartikel*
The *editor* analyses ...	*Herausgeber, Redakteur*
• The article presents an *interview* with ... which he / she gave in 1994.	*Interview*
• Mr ... is *interviewed* by a journalist (of the Daily Mail) about ...	*interviewen*
• The reporter encourages him to express his views on / about *clearly.*	*deutlich*
• The article is a *report* on ...	*Reportage, Bericht*
The report gives *background information* on / about ...	*Hintergrundinformationen*

The article gives an *account* of last week's events.	*Bericht*
a *survey* of	*Überblick, Übersicht*
• The report also contains a news *summary*.	*Zusammenfassung*
The author presents the events *in chronological order*.	*in chronologischer Reihenfolge*

• The author has a *conversation* with / to sb about / of ...	*Unterhaltung, Gespräch*
• The conversation *is about* ...	*handeln von*
• The author *talks* with / to sb about / of sth.	*sprechen, sich unterhalten*
• He *speaks* with / to sb about / of sth.	
The article reveals the standpoints of the *people taking part in the conversation*.	*Gesprächsteilnehmer*

The *graph* shows a certain development.	*Schaubild*
diagram	*graphische Darstellung*
The graph shows that the *percentage* has risen from ... % to ... % (in ten years).	*Prozentsatz*
The *statistics on* ... show that ...	*Statistik über*
The *statistical data* show that ...	*statistische Daten*

4.2. Der Werbetext *(the advertisement)*

4.2.1. Die drucktechnische Gestaltung *(the design and the lay-out)*

• *advertising*	*Werbung*
• The firm *advertises* ...	*werben für*
• The *advertisement*	*Werbetext*
• consists of the *headline*.	*Überschrift*
• the *(advertising) text*.	*(Werbe)Text*
• a *slogan*.	*Werbeslogan*
• a photo.	
• a picture.	
a *drawing*.	*Zeichnung*
• *At the top* of the page there is a photo showing...	*oben*
• *At the bottom*	*unten*
• *Above* the photo there is the headline, which presents the product.	*über, oberhalb*
• *Below*	*unter, unterhalb*
• The text is *illustrated* with photos.	*bebildert*

4.2.2. Die Textgestaltung *(the form and the contents of the text)*

• The text gives *information* on / about	*Informationen*
• the product.	
• the quality of the product.	
• the *use*	*Verwendung*
• the price	

The information about the product is objective.	
is *detailed.*	*ausführlich*
• This information *makes it possible* for the reader	*ermöglichen*
to form an exact idea	*sich eine genaue Vorstellung machen*
of the product.	
The information *is not sufficient*	*nicht ausreichen*
to form an exact idea of the product.	
The text does *not* give *any details* about ...	*nichts Genaues*
• There is a *relation(ship)* between the heading and the text. With regard to the *connection* between the picture and the text,	*Beziehung*
you can say that ...	
• The picture *draws* people's *attention*	*Aufmerksamkeit lenken auf*
to the product.	
Advertising works through *suggestion.*	*Suggestion*
• The photo *suggests* that the product is exclusive.	*suggerieren*
This advertisement has a great *power of suggestiveness.*	*Suggestivkraft*
• The slogan makes the *consumer* buy the product.	*Verbraucher*
• The slogan appeals to the consumer's *desire* for (youth).	*Verlangen*
sense of (beauty).	*Sinn für*
• The slogan *underlines* the positive aspects of the product.	*hervorheben*
The slogan *is related to* the picture.	*... ist bezogen auf*
The author uses several *techniques of persuasion.*	*Überredungstechniken*
• He *praises* the advantages of the product.	*preisen, rühmen*
• The text contains several	
• *statements* which the reader can easily believe.	*Behauptung*
• *promises*	*Versprechen*
• The name of the product is written in *capitals*	*Großbuchstabe*
• in order to *attract* the reader's *attention.*	*Aufmerksamkeit erregen*
• The author uses *superlatives* with the purpose	*Superlativ*
of suggesting *exclusiveness.*	*Exklusivität*
• Using the *comparative* " ...", the author pretends that	*Komparativ*
other products are *of inferior quality.*	*von minderer Qualität*
The *technical terms* are supposed to underline	*Fachausdrücke*
• the *excellent* quality of the product.	*erstklassig*
• The *choice of words* evokes an impression of	*Wortwahl*
• *luxury.*	*Luxus*
• good *taste.*	*Geschmack*
• The reader is *influenced* by the choice of words.	*beeinflussen*
• *manipulated*	*manipulieren*
He feels that the text *concerns* him directly.	*betreffen*
• By using imperatives, the author makes the reader believe	
that he ought to *possess* the article.	*besitzen*

By employing the personal pronoun "you", the author addresses the *potential buyer* directly.	*potentieller Käufer*
The use of the pronoun "we" suggests that	
• the author *identifies* with the reader.	*sich identifizieren*
The advertisement *presents ... as* a pleasant person	*darstellen als*
so that the reader can easily identify with him.	
• The text contains *emotional* expressions,	*affektiv, emotional*
• *for example* when the author says ...	*zum Beispiel*
This *paradoxical* formulation arouses the reader's curiosity.	*paradox*
• The text contains several *repetitions*.	*Wiederholung*
• The short and *incomplete* sentences give the text	*unvollständig*
its *rhythmic(al)* pattern.	*rhythmisch*

4.2.3. Die Zielsetzung des Werbetextes *(the purpose of the advertisement)*

• The advertisement addresses | *uncritical* | people.	*unkritisch*
| *cultivated* |	*kultiviert*
• | *(un)educated* |	*(un)gebildet*
| young |	

• The author wants to *awaken* the reader's *interest*	*Interesse wecken*
• in the product advertised.	
He *attempts to* influence the consumer's behaviour.	*versuchen*
He tries to manipulate the consumer's *subconscious*.	*Unterbewusstsein*
• He tries to *lead* the consumer *to* buy the product.	*dazu bringen*

He aims to arouse the reader's *secret desires*.	*geheime Wünsche*
• The author appeals to *the* reader's *desire for*	*der Wunsch nach*
| beauty.	
| youth.	
• | *health*.	*Gesundheit*
• | *security*.	*Sicherheit*
• | *success*.	*Erfolg*
• | *happiness*.	*Glück*
He appeals to the reader's desire to *increase*	*steigern, vergrößern*
his / her *social prestige*.	*Sozialprestige*
• It is the author's objective to *create* new desires.	*schaffen*

• The author wants to *make* the reader *believe* that ...	*glauben machen*
• He wants the reader to *become aware* of sth / that ...	*sich bewusst werden*
The advertisement *suggests* to the consumer that ...	*suggerieren*
Advertising presents an *idealized* world.	*idealisiert*

4.3. Die politische Rede *(the political speech)*

4.3.1. Die Position des Redners *(the speaker's standpoint)*

• He is a marvellous *speaker*. He is a fine political *orator*.	*Redner*
to *speak in public*	*öffentlich sprechen*
• The speaker *gives / makes a speech* on / about ...	*eine Rede halten*
He gives an *election speech*.	*Wahlrede*
He gives a *televised speech*.	*Fernsehansprache*
He gives a *radio address / radio speech*.	*Rundfunkansprache*
The speaker *openly* shows his interests.	*offen*
He speaks as a *representative* of a political party.	*Vertreter*
• The speaker *explains* the programme of his party.	*erläutern*
• He *defends* the party's *objectives*.	*verteidigen; Ziel*
He belongs to an *interest group*.	*Interessengruppe*
He *supports the interests* of ...	*die Interessen vertreten*
The speaker points out his own *merits*.	*Verdienste*
• He underlines the positive aspects of his *attitude*.	*Standpunkt*
• He *simplifies* the facts.	*vereinfachen*
He *distorts* the facts.	*verdrehen, verzerren*
He *blames* others *for* his *failures*.	*verantwortlich machen für; Fehler*
• The use of the pronoun "we" shows that the speaker identifies with the *audience*.	*Publikum*
• The speaker *appeals to* the listeners' feelings.	*appellieren an*
• He appeals to their emotions rather than to *reason*.	*Verstand*
He appeals to their *sense of responsibility*.	*Verantwortungsbewusstsein*

4.3.2. Die Position des Gegners *(the opponent's position)*

• The speaker has a good opinion of / about his *opponent*.	*Gegner*
He *recognizes* the positive aspects of the *opposing* viewpoints.	*anerkennen*; *gegnerisch*
• He *praises* his opponent's merits.	*loben*
He uses very positive expressions when he talks about him.	
• He *admits* that his opponent is right to say that ...	*zugeben, einräumen*
The speaker stresses the negative aspects of his opponent's views.	
He *diminishes* the positive aspects of his adversary's opinions.	*abschwächen*
• He *exaggerates* the *mistakes* his opponent made.	*übertreiben; Fehler*
He characterizes his adversary in negative terms.	
• He *attacks* his opponent openly.	*angreifen*
He *contests* his merits.	*bestreiten*
He *misrepresents* his adversary's statements.	*falsch wiedergeben*

He *distorts* his adversary's arguments.	*verdrehen, verzerren*
He *launches into a polemic* against ...	*in Polemik verfallen*

4.3.3. Die Ziele des Redners *(the speaker's aims)*

• The speaker tries to *influence* the audience.	*beeinflussen*
He wants the listeners to *adopt* his opinion.	*übernehmen*
He wants to *impose* his opinion *on* the listeners.	*aufzwingen*
He wants to win the listeners' *support* for ...	*Unterstützung*
• He aims to *get* the listeners *to* act.	*dazu bringen*
He aims to *mobilize* the people to take action.	*mobilisieren*
• He aims to *create a feeling* of solidarity.	*ein Gefühl schaffen*
His aim is to *spread propaganda* for his programme.	*Propaganda machen*
He intends to *give* his party *publicity*.	*bekannt machen*
• It is his intention to attack his opponent's *ideological* position.	*ideologisch*

4.3.4. Die sprachliche Gestaltung der Rede *(the language used in the speech)*

The speaker uses *techniques of persuasion*.	*Überredungstechniken*
He has a great *skill* in / at choosing his words.	*Geschick*
He is a great *stylist*.	*Meister des Stils*
His *speech level* is *elevated*.	*Sprachniveau; gehoben*
• His language is *clear*.	*klar*
He uses language of extraordinary *density*.	*Dichte*
His style is *concise*.	*prägnant, knapp*
He uses *emotive* language.	*affektiv, emotional*
He employs precise *formulations*.	*Formulierung*
• These expressions have a strong *effect* on the listener.	*Wirkung*
• He uses stereotyped / stereotypical *expressions*.	*Ausdruck*
• His style is *full of clichés*.	*voller Klischees*
His speech is full of aggressive *catch(-)phrases*.	*Schlagwort*
• His speech is full of *political slogans*.	*politischer Slogan*
• His speech is full of polemic(al) *statements*.	*Äußerung*
• His speech is full of ironic(al) *remarks*.	*Bemerkung*
The speaker uses a *vague form of wording*	*vage Formulierung*
so that everyone can interpret his statements	
• *according to* his own point of view.	*gemäß, nach*
• The speaker does not *state clearly*	*klar sagen, präzisieren*
• what he *means by* ...	*verstehen unter*
• how he understands ...	
These terms have negative *associations* for ...	*Assoziationen*

The sentences are only *juxtaposed.*	*aneinander gereiht*
• The speaker often employs *imperatives.*	*Imperativ*
The *frequent* use of imperatives underlines the urgent appeal (which is) aimed at the listeners.	*häufig*

5. DER STIL *(the style)*

5.1. Allgemeines *(general remarks)*

• The author's style is | *simple.*	*einfach*
| *varied.*	*abwechslungsreich*
| *vivid.*	*lebendig, anschaulich*
• His writing is | *abstract.*	*abstrakt*
• | *concrete.*	*konkret*
His statements are | *concise.*	*prägnant, knapp*
| have *appellative* function.	*appellativ*
• The text contains *descriptive* elements.	*deskriptiv*
The *stylistic diversity* shows in the use of ...	*abwechslungsreicher Stil*
The *simplicity* of style becomes apparent	*Einfachheit*
• in the *lack* of ...	*Fehlen*
• Several *elements of the text*	*Textelement*
• belong to | *literary language.*	*literarische Sprache*
| *(the) elevated style.*	*gehobener Stil*
• They are | characteristic of | *spoken English.*	*gesprochenes Englisch*
• | typical of | *colloquial language.*	*Umgangssprache*
• The author uses | *slang* | (words, expressions).	*Slang*
| *vulgar* |	*vulgär*
The *speech level* is rather elevated.	*Sprachebene*
This elevated style is in contrast with / to the *banality* of the contents.	*Banalität*
In the *narrative* parts, the author often uses literary language.	*narrativ*
• There are frequent *changes* from narrative parts to dialogues.	*Wechsel*
• The text is a *mixture* of elements taken from spoken language	*Mischung*
• and elements belonging to *written language.*	*geschriebene Sprache*
... is characterized by the vulgarity of	
• his *manner of speaking.*	*Sprechweise*
The simplicity of his speech *reflects* his naive way of thinking.	*widerspiegeln*
• His style is rather *technical.*	*technisch*
• He uses many *technical terms.*	*Fachausdruck*

• He always expresses his *thoughts* | in an abstract way.	*Gedanke*
• | *precisely*.	*präzise, genau*
• | in a *neutral* manner.	*neutral*
• He always remains *objective*.	*sachlich, objektiv*
• His way of speaking *corresponds with / to* his character.	*übereinstimmen mit*
• The text contains a lot of *direct speech*.	*direkte Rede*
The author uses direct speech in several places.	
The frequent use of direct speech gives the text *movement*.	*Lebendigkeit*
Exclamations occur rather frequently so that the tone of the text is quite *pathetic*.	*Ausruf* *pathetisch*
• The *atmosphere* created by the text is rather pessimistic.	*Atmosphäre*
The text is *predominantly* optimistic.	*vorwiegend*
An ironic(al) tone *predominates*.	*vorherrschen*
These *stylistic devices* | give the text its ironic(al) character.	*Stilmittel*
• | convey an idea of *impatience*.	*Ungeduld*

5.2. Der Wortschatz *(the vocabulary)*

• The *vocabulary* is technical.	*Wortschatz*
• The vocabulary contains many colloquial expressions.	
• Many words belong to *spoken language*.	*gesprochene Sprache*
• These expressions are *typical of* spoken laguage.	*typisch für*
• These words are *characteristic of* informal language.	*charakteristisch für*
The author has a *(marked) preference* for colloquialisms.	*(besondere) Vorliebe*
The author employs | *concise* formulations.	*prägnant, knapp*
| *meaningless* words.	*nichtssagend*
• This formulation is | *ironic(al).*	*ironisch*
| *paradoxical*.	*paradox*
• The vocabulary he uses contains many *technical terms*,	*Fachausdruck*
• which give the text its *scientific* character.	*wissenschaftlich*
• This | word | *expresses ...*	*ausdrücken*
term | *denotes ...*	*bezeichnen*
expression | *indicates ...*	*zeigen, hinweisen auf*
formulation | *illustrates ...*	*veranschaulichen*
• | *underlines ...*	*betonen, unterstreichen*
• | *alludes to ...*	*anspielen auf*
• This word has | a *negative meaning*.	*negative Bedeutung*
| negative *associations*.	*Assoziationen*
• This word *suggests* (loneliness).	*andeuten, denken lassen an*

With this word the author expresses the fact that ...	
• He *means by* this expression ...	*meinen mit, verstehen unter*
• This term *means* ...	*bedeuten*
This word is used *in the literal sense.*	*im wörtlichen Sinn*
in the figurative sense.	*im übertragenen Sinn*
This word has *(a) symbolic meaning.*	*symbolische Bedeutung*
This word has a *derogatory* meaning. / • This is a *pejorative* word.	*herabsetzend, abfällig*
• This word is a *synonym* for ...	*Synonym*
the *antonym* of ...	*Antonym*
• the *opposite* of ...	*Gegenteil*
• The author *defines* the word precisely.	*definieren*
• gives a *definition* of the term.	*Definition*
• In this passage there are two important *key words.*	*Schlüsselwort*
The key words of this text are ...	
The author uses a *diminutive*	*Verkleinerungsform*
in order to *moderate* his criticism of ...	*mildern*

5.3. Der Satzbau *(the sentence structure)*

• The *structure of the sentences* / • *sentence structure* / *syntactic structure* is very simple. / is varied.	*Satzbau*
• There are different *kinds* of sentences.	*Art, Typ*
• The *sentences* in general are rather short.	*Satz*
These short sentences do not always have a verb.	
• *imitate* spoken language.	*nachahmen*
produce a *lively* rhythm.	*lebhaft*
• sum up the author's *main theses.*	*Hauptthesen*
The sentences follow each other *in rapid succession.*	*in schneller Folge*
With the *accumulation* of short sentences, the author	*Häufung*
indicates the *quickness* of the action.	*Schnelligkeit*
• The *shortness* of the sentences expresses ...	*Kürze*
• The text contains many long and *complex* sentences,	*komplex*
• which produces a *slow* rhythm.	*langsam*
which underline the author's reflections on ...	
• The *length* of certain sentences indicates ...	*Länge*
• The *complexity* of the sentences corresponds with / to ...	*Komplexität*
The author *alternates* long sentences	*abwechselnd verwenden*
and / with very short ones.	
• The sentences are often *incomplete.* / *elliptic(al).*	*unvollständig*

The text consists of many incomplete sentences, which create an impression of *liveliness*.	*Lebhaftigkeit*
The sentences are merely *juxtaposed*.	*aneinander reihen*
• The sentences are not *connected with / to* each other.	*verknüpft mit*
There is no *logical connection* between the sentences.	*logische Verknüpfung*
The use of *paratactic(al)* structures *adds to* the author's statements.	*parataktisch, nebenordnend* / *Nachdruck verleihen*
• The sentences consist of several *subordinate clauses*.	*Nebensatz*
The use of *hypotactic(al)* structures gives the text *density*.	*hypotaktisch, unterordnend* / *Dichte*
There is (a) *disproportion* of / between the number of *main clauses* and subordinate clauses.	*Missverhältnis* / *Hauptsatz*
• The *lack* of subordinate clauses is characteristic of informal language.	*Fehlen*
The *causal clauses*, which are often used in this text, indicate ...	*Kausalsatz*
The *temporal clauses* / The *conditional clauses* show ...	*Temporalsatz* / *Konditionalsatz*
There is *syntactic parallelism* between these two sentences.	*syntaktischer Parallelismus*
• The *repetition* of certain syntactic elements suggests ...	*Wiederholung*
• With the help of *punctuation marks*, the author divides the text into several parts, so that the presentation of his thoughts is livelier and more interesting.	*Satzzeichen*
• *Dots* (...) indicate that words have been omitted.	*Auslassungszeichen*
• The reader has to *draw conclusions* about what has been left out.	*Schlussfolgerungen ziehen*
• *Exclamation marks* stress the emotions which are expressed in the text.	*Ausrufungszeichen*
• The sentence begins with a *causal conjunction*.	*kausale Konunktion*
The sentence ends with a *question mark*.	*Fragezeichen*
The sentence is preceded by ...	*dem Satz geht ... voraus.*
The sentence is followed by ...	*dem Satz folgt ...*

5.4. Die Grammatik *(grammar)*

• a *sentence*	*Satz*
• a *clause*	*Teilsatz*
• a *main clause*	*Hauptsatz*
• a *subordinate clause* / *subclause*	*Nebensatz*
dependent clause	*abhängiger Satz*
• a *relative clause*	*Relativsatz*
an *interrogative sentence*	*Fragesatz*
• a (*direct*) *question*	*direkte Frage*
an *interrogative clause*	*indirekter Fragesatz*
a *reported question*	*indirekte Frage*
• *direct speech*	*direkte Rede*
• *reported speech*	*indirekte Rede*
a *causal clause* / *clause of reason*	*Kausalsatz*
• a *conditional sentence*	*Bedingungssatzgefüge*
a *conditional clause* / • an *if-clause*	*Bedingungssatz*
a *temporal clause* / *clause of time*	*Temporalsatz*
a *concessive clause* / *clause of concession*	*Konzessivsatz, Einräumungssatz*
• the *subject*	*Subjekt*
• the *verb*	*Verb*
• the *word order*	*Satzstellung, Wortstellung*
the normal word order	
an *unusual* word order	*ungewöhnlich*
the *inversion* of the normal word order	*Umstellung*
the inversion of the verb	
the *inverted* form of the verb	*umstellen*
• a *direct object*	*direktes Objekt*
• an *indirect object*	*indirektes Objekt*
an *adverbial phrase*	*adverbiale Bestimmung*
an *adverbial expression*	*adverbialer Ausdruck*
of place	*des Ortes*
of time	*der Zeit*
• a *noun*	*Nomen, Substantiv*
• an *adjective*	*Adjektiv*
All the nouns in this paragraph have adjectives.	
Adjectives *come before* their noun.	*stehen vor*
This adjective is placed in an *unusual* position.	*ungewöhnlich*
The *participle is put after* the noun.	*Partizip; stehen nach*

• the *comparative*	*Komparativ*
The adjective is used in the comparative form.	
• the *superlative*	*Superlativ*
The *superlative* expressions underline ...	*superlativisch*
• an *adverb* | *of place*	*Ortsadverb*
• | *of time*	*Zeitadverb*
a *sentence adverb*	*Satzadverb*
• a *preposition*	*Präposition*
• a *conjunction*	*Konjunktion*
a *co(-)ordinating conjunction*	*beiordnende Konjunktion*
a *subordinating conjunction*	*unterodnende Konjunktion*
a | causal conjunction ("because")	
| conjunction of reason	
a | conditional conjunction ("if", "unless")	
| conjunction of condition	
a | temporal conjunction ("when", "after", "before")	
| conjunction of time	
• In this paragraph the author uses different *tenses*.	*Tempus*
• He often uses the | *present tense.*	*Präsens*
• | *past tense.*	*Imperfekt, Präteritum*
The present tense *predominates.*	*vorherrschen*
The largest part of the text is written in the past tense.	
In line 10, | *the tense changes.*	*das Tempus wechselt*
| there is a *change of tense.*	*Tempuswechsel*
The author *changes* from the present to the past tense.	*wechseln*
In the dialogues, the verbs are in the present tense, and in the narrative parts, they are in the past tense.	
The author *almost exclusively* uses the present tense.	*fast ausschließlich*
the | *pluperfect* / • | *past perfect*	*Plusquamperfekt*
• This passage is written in the *future tense.*	*Futur*
• the *conditional*	*Konditional*
• the | *continuous* / • | *progressive* | *form* of the verb	*Verlaufsform*
In this text, the past continuous is used for the description of the *background* to the story.	*Hintergrund*
The past progressive refers to a longer background action or situation.	
• The past simple refers to the *events* related in the story.	*Ereignis*
The story is told in the past simple.	
• the *singular*	*Singular*
• the *plural*	*Plural*

The verb is in the singular.
The subject is plural.

- the *third person singular* — *3. Person Singular*
- the first person *pronoun* — *Pronomen*
- the *imperative* — *Imperativ*

The frequent use of imperatives shows that the text is an appeal directed to the reader.

- a difficult grammatical *construction* — *Konstruktion*
- a | that-construction / that-clause / that-structure
- an | *infinitive* construction / infinitive-structure — *Infinitiv*
- *modal auxiliaries* — *modale Hilfsverben*
- the *gerund* — *Gerundium*
- a *participle* — *Partizip*
- the *present participle* — *Partizip Präsens*
- the *past participle* — *Partizip Perfekt*

The frequent occurrence of participles contributes to the *conciseness* of the text. — *Knappheit, Prägnanz*

- the *active (voice)* — *Aktiv*

The author uses mainly active verbs.
The sentence is active.

- the *passive (voice)* — *Passiv*

The verbs are used in the passive.
It is a passive sentence.
an *impersonal* | verb / sentence — *unpersönlich*
an it-construction

- These are *negative* sentences. — *verneint*

an *affirmative* sentence — *bejaht*

5.5. Die Stilmittel *(the stylistic devices)*

- a *stylistic* | *device*
- | *means* } — *Stilmittel*

The author uses certain stylistic devices in order to
| awaken the reader's interest.
| persuade the reader to adopt his opinion.

- the *repetition* — *Wiederholung*

The repetition of the word stresses ...

- The author *repeats* this word over and over again. — *wiederholen*

• an *enumeration*	*Aufzählung*
This sentence contains an enumeration of (verbs).	
• The author *enumerates* ...	*aufzählen*
the *intensification*	*Steigerung*
In this enumeration you can notice the gradual intensification of feelings.	
an *accumulation*	*Häufung*
This sentence contains an accumulation of adjectives, which shows that ...	
• a *comparison*	*Vergleich*
The author draws a comparison between ...	
He *compares* ... with / to ...	*vergleichen*
... is compared with / to ...	
• an *image*	*(sprachliches) Bild*
This image expresses a strong feeling of (loneliness).	
• The images have (a) *symbolic meaning.* / *symbolic significance.*	*symbolische Bedeutung*
• a *metaphor for*	*Metapher für*
This metaphor expresses ...	
This sentence contains a *metaphorical* expression.	*metaphorisch*
• a *symbol of*	*Symbol für*
(The rose) is a symbol of (love).	
(The rose) *symbolizes* / *stands for* (love).	*symbolisieren* / *stehen für*
parallelism	*Parallelismus*
There is syntactic parallelism between these two sentences.	
• These two sentences have a *parallel* structure.	*parallel*
an *antithesis*	*Antithese*
This expression is the complete antithesis of ...	
These sentences have an *antithetical* structure.	*antithetisch*
an *exclamation*	*Ausruf*
The sentence begins with an exclamation.	
• a *rhetorical question*	*rhetorische Frage*
The author often asks rhetorical questions.	
• the *personification* of	*Personifizierung*

This is a personification of (the machine).
• In this sentence the author *personifies* (the machine). — *personifizieren*

• an *allusion* — *Anspielung*
This sentence contains an allusion to ...
• The author *alludes to* ... — *anspielen auf*

• *irony* — *Ironie*
The text contains irony.
The author says with heavy irony that ...
• The text is *ironic(al).* — *ironisch*

a *paraphrase of* — *Umschreibung für*
The author uses a paraphrase when he talks about (happiness).

an *example of anaphora* — *eine Anapher*
This passage presents several examples of anaphora.
These *anaphoral* expressions underline ... — *anaphorisch*

• a *euphemism* — *Euphemismus*
When talking about (war), the author employs
| a euphemism.
| a *euphemistic* expression — *euphemistisch*

an *apostrophe* — *Apostrophe*
The beginning of the text is an apostrophe to (nature).
The poet *apostrophizes* (nature). — *apostrophieren*

6. AUSDRÜCKE ZUR ABFASSUNG EINES TEXTKOMMENTARS *(expressions useful for writing comments)*

6.1. Seine persönliche Meinung äußern *(to give one's personal opinion)*

• I *think* / I *consider* | that ... — *denken*
• I *believe* that ... — *glauben*
I *consider* sth | (to be) ... / *as* ... — *ansehen als, betrachten*
• I *am of* / I *have* / I *hold* / I *take* | *the opinion* that ... / *the view* that ... — *der Meinung sein*

- *in my opinion / view ...*, *to my mind ...* — *meiner Meinung nach*
- My *opinion of / about* this subject is that ... / My *view on / about* this point is that ... — *Meinung über*
- I have the *impression* that ... — *Eindruck*
  My (personal) impression of this is ....

- *So far as I know ...*
- *As far as I know ...* — *soweit / soviel ich weiß*
  to my knowledge, ... — *meines Wissens*
  to my experience, ... — *meiner Erfahrung nach*
  I know *from experience* that ... — *aus Erfahrung*
  If I am not mistaken, ... — *wenn ich mich nicht irre*
  If I remember rightly / correctly, ... — *wenn ich mich recht erinnere*

- I am *convinced* of ... / that ... — *überzeugt*
- I am *certain* that ...
- I am *sure* about / of ... — *sicher*
  I am not certain / I am not sure — who / what / how ... / if / whether ...
- I do not know *exactly* ... — *genau*
- I have *doubts* about ... — *Zweifel*
- I *doubt* that ... — *bezweifeln*

- It seems / It is *possible* that ... — *möglich*
- It seems / It is *impossible* that ... — *unmöglich*
  I find it impossible to ...
- It seems / It is *probable* / *likely* that ... — *wahrscheinlich*
- It seems / It is *improbable* / *unlikely* that ... — *unwahrscheinlich*
  not very likely — *wenig wahrscheinlich*
  rather unlikely — *ziemlich unwahrscheinlich*
- ... is *probably* afraid of (loneliness). — *wahrscheinlich* (Adv.)

- It *appears* / It *seems* that ... / as if / as though ... / to be ... — *(er)scheinen*
  It seems to me that ...
  It seems difficult for the author to ...
  It seems to me (to be) the best solution to ...
  The author seems to ...

6.2. Mit dem Autor einverstanden sein *(to agree with the author)*

• I *am of the same opinion as* the author. / • I *agree* with the author.	*derselben Meinung sein*
I agree with the author on / about this point. / on / about this question.	
I agree with the author's analysis of ... / with what the author says about ...	
• The author *is right* about ... / to criticize ...	*Recht haben*
He is completely right when he says that ...	
• *From a psychological point of view,* the author is right.	*vom psychologischen Standpunkt aus*
In a sense the author is right.	*in gewissem Sinne*
In a (certain) way the author is right.	*in gewisser Weise*
What the author says about ... is true *to some extent.*	*bis zu einem gewissen Grade*
• The author *has reason to* believe ...	*Grund haben zu*

6.3. Den Autor kritisieren, nicht einverstanden sein *(to criticize the author, to disagree)*

• I *am not of the same opinion as* the author. / • I *disagree with* the author.	*anderer Meinung sein*
• I disagree / I do not agree with the author on / about this point. / with what the author says about ...	
• My opinion *is* very *different from* the author's.	*anders sein als*
• The author *is* completely *wrong* about ... / • to criticize ...	*Unrecht haben*
• I consider it (to be) *wrong* to say that ...	*falsch*
• In my opinion / In my view / To my mind it is wrong / *it is a mistake* to say ... / to believe ...	*ein Fehler sein*
I think that the author *is mistaken* when he says ...	*sich irren*
The author *commits an error* when he says ...	*einen Irrtum begehen*
Contrary to the author, I am of the opinion ...	*im Gegensatz zu*
• I *ask myself* if / whether ...	*sich fragen*
• I don't *understand* why ...	*verstehen*
The author does not *give the impression* of wanting ...	*den Eindruck erwecken*
• This idea cannot be *taken seriously.*	*ernst nehmen*

I would like to *clarify* some details which the author mentions in connection with ...	*klarstellen*
Some aspects still have to be clarified.	
• I'd like to *comment on* the author's statements about ...	*kommentieren*
• There is a *contradiction* in what the author says on the subject of ...	*Widerspruch*
• These two statements are *contradictory*.	*widersprüchlich*
• The first statement *contradicts* the second.	*widersprechen*
• The author's opinion *stands in contrast to* ... / His opinion *contrasts* with ...	*im Gegensatz stehen zu*
• This statement is *contrasted* with ...	*gegenüberstellen*
• The author contrasts it with ...	
• These two standpoints cannot be *compared*.	*vergleichen*
They *are* not *comparable*.	*vergleichbar*
They are *incompatible* with ...	*unvereinbar*

6.4. Auf eine Notwendigkeit hinweisen *(to point out the necessity of something)*

• It has to be *pointed out that* ...	*darauf hinweisen, dass ...*
• *Nevertheless*, / • *However*, you can also say that ...	*jedoch, dennoch*
• I must nevertheless / still *add* that ...	*hinzufügen*
If you *examine* this problem *more closely*,	*genauer betrachten*
• you will *realize* ...	*feststellen*
• If you *think carefully about* this question,	*gründlich nachdenken über*
• you will *become aware* of the fact that ...	*sich bewusst werden*
• It should be *taken into consideration* / *taken into account* / • *considered* that ...	*bedenken*
After all, it has to be *recognized* that ...	*anerkennen, berücksichtigen*
• I would like to *draw attention to* the fact that ...	*aufmerksam machen auf*
• I must *stress* / *emphasize* / • *underline* that ...	*betonen*
I want to *make it clear that* ...	*deutlich machen, dass ...*
• I want to *state clearly* that ...	*klar sagen*
• However, I *ask myself* how ...	*sich fragen*
• It ought to be *mentioned* that ...	*erwähnen*
• It should be *remembered* that ...	*daran denken*
• One must not *forget* that ...	*vergessen*

6.5. Weitere Ausdrücke der persönlichen Stellungnahme
(further expressions used to state one's own opinion)

(So,) *in summary*, / • (So,) *to sum up*, — you can say that ... / one can say that ...	*zusammenfassend*
• *On the whole*, / • *All in all*, — you can say that ... / one can say that ...	*insgesamt, alles in allem*
• *Generally speaking*, — you can say that ... / one can say that ...	*ganz allgemein gesagt*
• It is *obvious* / *evident* that ...	*offensichtlich, klar*
It is *apparent* that ...	*einleuchtend*
It goes without saying that ...	*es versteht sich von selbst*
It stands to reason that ...	*es leuchtet jedem ein*
• *The same is true of* ...	*dasselbe gilt für*
• *It is the same with* ...	*es ist dasselbe bei*
• *This is similar to* ...	*es verhält sich ähnlich mit*
This *amounts to the same thing.*	*auf dasselbe hinauslaufen*
• This *has nothing to do with* ...	*nichts zu tun haben mit*
• *It is no use* (protesting against ...)	*es nützt nichts*
• It is true that ..., but *strictly speaking*, ...	*genau genommen*
• This seems to be true, but *in fact* ...	*tatsächlich, eigentlich*
• It is not my *intention* to (criticize ...)	*Absicht*
I do not *intend* to (criticize ...)	*beabsichtigen*
• *The most important thing* is ...	*das Wichtigste*
• *What is important is* ... / *It is essential* *that* ... / to do sth	*wichtig ist, dass ...*
• *It does not matter*, why / what / how ...	*es spielt keine Rolle*
• *What* really *matters is* ... / *What counts* here *is* (how you act).	*was zählt, ist ...*
• This is of no *importance* (at all). / *significance* for ...	*Bedeutung*
The principal / main / chief goal / objective / aim *consists in* (convincing...) / must be (to convince ...)	*darin bestehen*
This *raises the question* as to why ...	*die Frage aufwerfen*
The question arises as to why ...	*die Frage stellt sich*
• *The real problem* is that ...	*das eigentliche Problem*
• This *implies* that ...	*bedeuten, mit sich bringen*

Provided / *Supposing* / *Assuming* (*that*) ...	*vorausgesetzt, dass ...*
One could *suppose* / *assume* / *presume* (that) ...	*annehmen, vermuten*
• What *strikes* me *above all* ...	*auffallen; besonders*
What strikes me *particularly* ... / *especially* ...	*besonders*
• What is *strange* is the fact that ...	*merkwürdig*
One could *go (one step) further* and ask ...	*(einen Schritt) weitergehen*
• The author *conveys* / *produces* / *gives* *the impression* that ...	*den Eindruck vermitteln*
• The reader *gets* / *has* *the impression* that ...	*den Eindruck bekommen*
• It is not necessary to *go into detail(s).*	*in die Einzelheiten gehen*
• *The result of this is ...*	*daraus ergibt sich / folgt, dass ...*
• *As a* / *In* *consequence of this, ...*	*als Folge davon*
• *One thing is certain*:	*soviel steht fest:*
I *can say for certain* that ...	*sicher sagen können*

6.6. Wortschatz zum Textzusammenhang *(vocabulary referring to the composition of the text)*

6.6.1. Den Text gliedern *(to subdivide the text)*

• *First(ly),* / *In the first place,* / *First of all,* I am going to summarize the text.	*zuerst*
• I'll *begin with* / I'll *start with* a summary of the text.	*anfangen mit*
• *At the beginning*, I'm going to deal with the problem of ...	*am Anfang*
• *Then* / *After that,* / *Afterwards,* I would like to introduce the subject of ... / discuss the problem of ... / raise the question of ...	*dann, danach*
The next step in the argumentation has to be to analyse the behaviour of ...	*der nächste Schritt*
Now we should *proceed to* / *pass on to* the analysis of ... / the examination of ...	*übergehen zu*

- Now *let's* examine the question of whether ... — *wir wollen*

- *Finally,* / *Lastly,* / *In conclusion,* I would like to say ... — *zum Schluss* / *abschließend*

  I would like to conclude by saying ... — *abschließend möchte ich sagen*

6.6.2. Auf Textstellen verweisen *(to refer to passages of the text)*

- I (have) already mentioned *(further) above* ... — *(weiter) oben*
  In the *above(-mentioned)* paragraph I pointed out ... — *oben genannt*
- *see above / below* — *siehe oben / unten*
- I will discuss this problem *(further) below.* — *(weiter) unten*
- I would like to *come back to* this point in the following / next paragraph. — *zurückkomen auf*
- I want to *take up* the problem *again* which I have already dealt with in the preceding paragraph. / in one of the paragraphs above. — *wieder aufnehmen*
- I am going to *deal with* this question only *briefly.* — *kurz abhandeln*

- *Before* I proceed to analyse ... I want to talk briefly about / of ... — *bevor*
- *After* analysing (the behaviour of ...) I would like to raise the problem of (unemployment). — *nachdem*

- (In order) to understand the author's attitude, let's *look at an example.* — *ein Beispiel betrachten*
- (In order) to illustrate the present situation, I will *quote ... as an example.* — *als Beispiel nennen*

- Let's enter into a *detailed* discussion of ... — *detailliert*
- Let's discuss this *in detail.* — *im Detail*
- Let's *think again about* the author's attitude towards ... — *erneut betrachten*

6.6.3. Die Reihenfolge der Gedanken angeben *(to indicate the sequence of ideas)*

- *At the beginning of the text,...*
- *First(ly), ...* / *In the first place, ...* / *First of all, ...* — *zuerst*

- *Afterwards, …*
- *After that, …*
- *Then …*

dann, danach

- *Additionally, ...*
- *In addition, ...*
- *Moreover, ...*
- *Also, ...*
- *Besides, ...*

außerdem

- I would like to *add* that ... — *hinzufügen*
- *There is an additional problem.* — *Hinzu kommt ein weiteres Problem.*
- *Another problem is ...* — *ein weiteres Problem ist ...*

- *At the end*, / *Finally*, / *Lastly*, — I would like to say ... — *zum Schluss*
- *In conclusion*, — *abschließend*
- *In summary*, / *To sum up*, — *zusammenfassend*
- *I would like to conclude by saying ...* — *abschließend möchte ich sagen...*

6.6.4. Seinen Standpunkt erläutern / präzisieren *(to explain / state one's point of view clearly)*

- *That is (to say) ...* — *das heißt ...*
- *By this I mean ...* — *damit will ich sagen ...*
- This *means* / *signifies* ... — *heißen, bedeuten*
- *This doesn't mean that ...* — *das bedeutet nicht, dass ...*
- *In other words ...* — *mit anderen Worten*
- *To put it in another way ...* — *um es anders auszudrücken*
- I'd *rather* say that ... — *eher, vielmehr*

6.6.5. Zeitangaben machen *(to indicate the time)*

6.6.5.1. Gegenwart *(the present)*

- *today* — *heute*
- *now* — *jetzt*
- *at the moment* — *im Augenblick*
- *at present* / *presently* / *at the present time* — *gegenwärtig*
- *for the moment* — *im Augenblick, vorübergehend*

currently	*zur Zeit*
• *nowadays* / *these days*	*heutzutage*
• *the present (time)*	*die Gegenwart*
We live in the present.	
the modern age	*die heutige Zeit*
• *up to now* / • *until now* / • *till now*	*bis jetzt*
up to / *up until* *the present (day)*	*bis heute*
• *from now on* / *as of now*	*von jetzt an*
• *from today onward(s)* / *as of today* / *as from today*	*von heute an*

6.6.5.2. Vergangenheit *(the past)*

• *at that time*	*in jener Zeit*
At the time when (he was born)	*damals, als*
• *at the time of* (the First World War)	*zur Zeit des/der*
in prehistoric times	*in prähistorischen Zeiten*
in ancient times	*in der Antike*
in Medieval times	*im Mittelalter*
in recent times	*in jüngster Vergangenheit*
in the days of (Shakespeare)	*zu Zeiten von*
in his day	*zu seiner Zeit*
• (one / a hundred and fifty) *years ago*	*vor* (150) *Jahren*
• *in the* (19th) *century*	*im* (19.) *Jahrhundert*
• *in (the year)* (2000)	*im Jahre* (2000)
• *in the (sixties)*	*in den (sechziger) Jahren*
• *during the past few years* / • *for the last few years* / • *in the last few years*	*in den letzten Jahren*
This problem was brought up *recently.*	*vor kurzem*
• It has been widely discussed *recently.* / *lately.*	*in der letzten Zeit*
formerly / • *in former times*	*früher*

• *the past (time)* These problems did not exist in the past.	*Vergangenheit*
• *on that day*	*an diesem / jenem Tag*
• *(just) at that moment* *at that precise moment*	*(gerade) in diesem / jenem Augenblick*
• *till that moment* *(up) until that moment*	*bis zu diesem / jenem Augenblick*
• *from this / that moment (on)*	*von diesem / jenem Augenblick an*
• *yesterday*	*gestern*
• *last week* / month / year	*vorige / letzte Woche*
• *(on) the day before* *(on) the previous day* *(on) the preceding day*	*am Tag davor*
• (*on*) *the day before* his departure	*am Tag vor ...*
(*on*) *the day before* he left	*am Tag, bevor ...*
• *(on) the day after* • *(on) the next day* • *(on) the following day*	*am folgenden / nächsten Tag*
• (*on*) *the day after* his arrival	*am Tag nach ...*
(*on*) *the day after* he arrived	*am Tag, nachdem ...*
• *the week before* • *the previous week* • *the preceding* week	*in der Woche davor*
• *the month before*	*im Monat davor*
• *the year before*	*im Jahr davor*
• two weeks *later*	*später*
• three days *after that*	*danach*
• *soon* | *after that* *shortly* | *thereafter* *not long* | *after*	*kurz danach*
• *a short time later*	*kurze Zeit später*

6.6.5.3. Zukunft *(the future)*

• the *future* (*time*)	*Zukunft*
a future age	*ein zukünftiges Zeitalter*
In the future, / In a future age, | there will be ...	
in the near future	*in naher Zukunft*
in the immediate future	*in unmittelbarer Zukunft*

in the distant future	*in ferner Zukunft*
• *tomorrow*	*morgen*
• *next week* / month / year	*nächste Woche*
• *in the next few years*	*in den nächsten Jahren*
in the years to come	*in den kommenden Jahren*

6.6.6. Gründe angeben *(to give reasons)*

• *This is why ...* • *Because of this ...*	*daher, deshalb, deswegen*
• *Because of* / *On account of* / *By reason of* — (this development) ... / (this difficulty, problem) ... / (his age) ...	*wegen, aufgrund*
• *the reason to do sth*	*der Grund, etw. zu tun*
• *the reason for (doing) sth*	*der Grund für*
The author's reason to say this is ...	
His reasons for saying this are ...	
There are various reasons for these statements.	
• *the reason why ...*	*der Grund, warum ...*
the reason is that ...	*der Grund ist, dass ...*
The reason (why) the author says so is ...	
The reasons the author says so are that ...	
• to *have* (every) *reason to* (believe ...)	*Grund haben*
to have no reason to ...	
• *to give a reason*	*einen Grund angeben*
• *For this reason ...*	*aus diesem Grund*
• *For the same reason ...*	*aus demselben Grund*
• *for (political) reasons*	*aus (politischen) Gründen*
for reasons of (safety)	*aus Gründen der (Sicherheit)*
• *for the following reasons ...*	*aus folgenden Gründen*
The reasons are *as follows:*	*wie folgt:*
the grounds to do sth	*berechtigte Gründe, etw. zu tun*
the grounds for (doing) sth	*berechtigte Gründe für*
to *have* good / no *grounds for ...*	*Gründe haben für*
to condemn sth *on (moral) grounds*	*aus (moralischen) Gründen*
on (the) grounds of ...	*wegen, aufgrund*
He refuses to accept this theory on the grounds of insufficient evidence.	
on the grounds that ...	*deswegen, weil ...*
He criticizes this attitude on the grounds that it is anti-social.	

- *the cause of sth* — *die Ursache von*
- *the cause for sth* — *die Ursache für*

  Poverty was the cause of the revolt.
  There is (no) cause for alarm.

the basic cause of ... — *die tiefere Ursache für*

6.6.7. Folgen aufzeigen *(to show consequences)*

Thus, ... — *daher, also*
Therefore, ... — *deshalb*
(in) this / that way — *auf diese Weise*
Hence ... — *daher, infolgedessen*
Accordingly, ... / *Consequently, ...* / *As a consequence (of this), ...* / *In consequence (of this), ...* — *folglich*
The *consequence* of (these measures) is ... — *Folge*
(These measures) *entail ...* — *nach sich ziehen*
(These measures) *result in ...* — *zur Folge haben*
This is a (direct) *result* of ... — *Ergebnis, Folge*
The result of this is ...

6.6.8. Den Gegensatz / Unterschied ausdrücken *(to express contrast / difference)*

- *but* — *aber*

in contrast, ... / *by contrast, ...* — *dagegen*

  The young generation is, in / by contrast, much more interested in environmental issues.

in contrast with / to ... / *unlike ...* / *contrary to ...* — *im Gegensatz zu*

  In contrast with / to the Americans, the British are ...

- *Nevertheless,* / *However,* / *Still,* / *Yet,* you can say that ... — *dennoch, trotzdem*
- You can nevertheless / still say ...

just the same ... / *all the same ...* — *dennoch, trotzdem*

  Just the same, the situation hasn't changed.
  The situation hasn't changed, all the same.

- *In spite of ...* / *Despite ...* — *trotz* (Präp.)

In spite of all his efforts, he failed.	
• *(Al)though ...* *(Even) though ...*	*obwohl* (Konj.)
(Al)though he tried very hard, he failed.	
He failed (even) though he tried very hard.	
on the contrary, ...	*im Gegenteil*
He did not lie. On the contrary, he told the truth.	

6.7. Weitere Ausdrücke für die Abfassung eines Textkommentars *(further expressions for writing a comment)*

in the field of politics	*im Bereich*
in the political field	
in the area of culture	*im Bereich*
in the cultural area	
in the sphere of medical science	*im Bereich*
in the scientific sphere	
in the domain of philosophy	*im Bereich*
in the world of the press	*in der Welt des / der ...*
in the business *world*	*in der ... Welt*
in the scientific world	
from a (social) point of view / viewpoint / standpoint	*aus (sozialer) Sicht*
from the viewpoint of (young people)	*vom Standpunkt (Jugendlicher) aus*
from this point of view	*aus dieser Sicht*
in this respect	*in dieser Hinsicht*
• *in comparison with / to ...*	*im Vergleich mit*
In comparison with / to the USA, the UK is ...	
compared with / to ...	*verglichen mit*
Compared with / to last year ...	
in relation to ...	*im Verhältnis zu*
In relation to the cost of living, earnings are low.	
• *as far as ... is / are concerned*	*was ... betrifft*
As far as the problems of immigrants are concerned ...	
as for ... *as to ...*	*was ... betrifft*
As for / to the immigration procedures ...	

as regards ...	*was ... betrifft*
As regards the restrictions on immigration ...	
• *As far as I am concerned,* / *As for me* I don't mind ...	*was mich betrifft*
For my part ...	*ich meinerseits*
Personally, I'd prefer ...	*ich persönlich*
• *on the one hand ..., on the other hand ...*	*einerseits ... , andererseits*
• *in theory* ..., but in reality ...	*in der Theorie*
• in theory ..., but *in practice*	*in der Praxis*
• *theoretically ... , but practically*	*theoretisch ..., aber praktisch*
• (the environment) *in general*	*im Allgemeinen*
• *Generally, ...*	*ganz allgemein*
Generally, you can say that ...	
• *Generally speaking, ...*	*im Allgemeinen*
Generally speaking, the air is mainly polluted by ...	
• *usually*	*gewöhnlich*
in any case / *at any rate*	*auf jeden Fall, jedenfalls*
in any event / *at all events*	*auf alle Fälle*
• *in this case*	*in diesem Fall*
in the present case	*im vorliegenden Fall*
not on any account / *on no account*	*keineswegs, auf keinen Fall*
by no means / *not by any means*	*keinesfalls, durchaus nicht*
• *in / under no circumstances*	*unter gar keinen Umständen*
in a word	*mit einem Wort*
• *briefly*	*kurz*
basically	*im Grunde, grundsätzlich*
as a matter of fact	*eigentlich*
I don't agree. As a matter of fact, I am strongly against the author's suggestions.	
• *in fact*	*eigentlich*
This is, in fact, what happened.	
in a sense / *in a (certain) way*	*in gewisser Weise*

- *in this respect* — *in dieser Hinsicht*
- *so to speak* — *sozusagen*
- *to be frank (with you)* / *(quite) frankly* / *to be honest* / *(quite) honestly* — *offen / ehrlich gesagt*
- *to tell (you) the truth* — *um die Wahrheit zu sagen*
- *strictly speaking, ...* — *genau genommen*

  Strictly speaking, the author is not English, but Scottish.

be that as it may — *wie dem auch sei*

7. DISKUSSIONSWORTSCHATZ
(vocabulary used in discussions)

I believe that ...
I think that ...
I believe so.
I think not.
I don't think so.
I am of the opinion that ...

In my opinion ... / To my mind ...
I've got the impression that ...

As far as I know ... / *To my knowledge ...* — *soviel ich weiß*
According to what I've been told ...
If I remember rightly, ...

I am convinced of / that ...
I am certain / I am sure — that ... / about / of ...
I am not certain if / whether ...
I don't know exactly if ... / why ... / when ...
I don't understand why ...

What do you think about / of ...?
What is your opinion about / of ...?
What are your views about / on ...?

I agree with you on / about this point.
I agree with what you say on the subject of ...
What X says about ... is true.

What you say about ... is right.
You are right about this.
I think that X is completely right to say ...
I completely agree with you as far as ... is concerned.
I am of the same opinion as you are.

I disagree with you on / about this point.
I disagree with what you say about ...
What X says about ... is not true.
What you say about ... is wrong.
I think it's wrong to say that ...
It's a *mistake* to believe ... *Irrtum*
I think that X *is mistaken* about ... *sich irren*
I am of a different opinion.

I would like to say ...
I only want to say ...
I wanted to say the same thing.
I wanted to say that, too.
As I've just said ...

One must say that ...
It has to be emphasized that ...
You have to add that ...
We have to ask ourselves why ...
} *man muss*
One mustn't forget that ...
One should also mention that ...
We have to *take into consideration* that ... / *bear in mind* that ... } *berücksichtigen*

I would like to correct what you've just said.
There is a *contradiction* in what you say. *Widerspruch*

I would like to come back to the point X has just made.
I want to return to what X said about ... a minute ago.
I would like to take X's argument up again.
I would like to *support* X in what he says. *unterstützen*
I would like to add another point.
I want to *raise a* further *problem*. *ein Problem anschneiden*
I want to draw your attention to the fact that ...

It is *evident* that ...
It is *obvious* that ...
} *offensichtlich, klar*
It goes without saying ... *es versteht sich von selbst*
It is the same with ... *es ist dasselbe bei*

The same is true of ...	*dasselbe gilt für*
This amounts to *the same (thing).* *This comes to the same.*	*das läuft aufs Gleiche hinaus*
This is *different.*	*anders*
That is (quite) another thing. *That is a different matter (altogether).*	*das ist (ganz) etwas anderes*
This has nothing to do with ...	*das hat nichts zu tun mit ...*
It is no use criticizing ... *It is no good* criticizing ...	*es nützt nichts*
The question is not whether ...	*es geht nicht darum, ob ...*
The point is that ...	*es geht darum, dass ...*
It is not my intention to (criticize ...)	*es geht mir nicht darum, ...*
The most important thing is ...	*das Wichtigste ist ...*
What is important is ...	*wichtig ist, dass ...*
This is of no importance.	
This is not the problem.	*das ist nicht das Problem*
The problem is to find out if ... *The problem is* that ...	*das Problem ist ...*
The question is, do we really need ...	*die Frage ist ...*
That is (to say), ...	
This means that ...	
This signifies that ...	
I mean by this ...	*damit meine ich ...*
This doesn't mean that ...	
I'd rather say ...	
How shall I put it?	*Wie soll ich sagen?*
In other words ...	*anders ausgedrückt*
To put it differently, ... *To put it in another way, ...*	*um es anders auszudrücken*
What is the meaning of ...?	*Was ist die Bedeutung von ...?*
What does ... mean?	*Was bedeutet ...?*
What do you mean by ...?	*Was verstehst du unter/ meinst du mit...?*
Could you please explain to me ...	
What strikes me particularly is the fact that ...	*was mir besonders auffällt*
For this reason ...	*aus diesem Grund*
It is for this reason that ...	
This is *the reason why ...*	*der Grund, warum ...*
The reason for this is ...	*der Grund dafür*

So, ... / *(In) this / that way ...*	*so, auf diese Weise*
Consequently, ...	*infolgedessen*
The consequence of this is ...	*die Folge davon ist ...*
This results from ...	*dies folgt aus ...*
This results in ...	*dies führt zu ...*
In contrast to that, ...	*dagegen, im Unterschied dazu*
Contrary to what is generally believed ...	*im Gegensatz zu*
As far as (the problem of pollution) *is concerned ...* / *As regards* (the pollution of the air) ...	*was ... betrifft*
As far as I am concerned ... / *As for me, ...* / *For my part ...*	*ich meinerseits*
On the one hand ..., on the other hand ...	*einerseits ..., andererseits ...*
In theory ..., but in reality ...	*in der Theorie ..., aber in Wirklichkeit*
Theoretically ..., but practically ...	*theoretisch ..., aber praktisch*
in the area of (politics) ... / *in the* (scientific) *field ...*	*im Bereich*
With regard to social problems ...	*hinsichtlich*
from a (social) point of view	*vom (sozialen) Standpunkt aus*
from the standpoint of (young people)	*vom Standpunkt (der Jugendlichen) aus*
in this respect	*in dieser Hinsicht*
in relation to ...	*im Verhältnis zu*
Generally, / *In general,* one can say ...	*im Allgemeinen, allgemein*
in any case / *at any rate*	*auf jeden Fall, jedenfalls*
in this case	*in diesem Fall*
at all events	*auf alle Fälle*
Briefly, ...	*kurz*
In a word ...	*mit einem Wort*
basically	*im Grunde, grundsätzlich*
in a (certain) way	*gewissermaßen, in gewisser Weise*
in a sense	*in gewissem Sinne*
in this respect	*in dieser Hinsicht*

at first sight	*auf den ersten Blick*
To tell (you) the truth, ...	*um die Wahrheit zu sagen*
Frankly, ... *Honestly, ...*	*ehrlich / offen gesagt*
Strictly speaking, ...	*genau genommen*

Deutsch-englisches Stichwortverzeichnis

Dieses Verzeichnis enthält nur die wichtigsten Stellenangaben. Die Ziffern verweisen auf die Seiten, auf denen das Stichwort vorkommt.

A

B

C

D

E

F

G

H

I

J

K

L

M

N

O

P

Q

R

S

T

U

V

W

Z